nolds Letters

An Irish Emigrant Family in
Late Victorian Manchester

IRISH NARRATIVES

IRISH NARRATIVES

Series edited by David Fitzpatrick

Personal narratives of past lives are essential for understanding any field of history. They provide unrivalled insight into the day-to-day consequences of political, social, economic or cultural relationships. Memoirs, diaries and personal letters, whether by public figures or obscure witnesses of historical events, will often captivate the general reader as well as engrossing the specialist. Yet the vast majority of such narratives are preserved only among the manuscripts or rarities in libraries and archives scattered over the globe. The aim of this series of brief yet scholarly editions is to make available a wide range of narratives concerning Ireland and the Irish over the last four centuries. All documents, or sets of documents, are edited and introduced by specialist scholars, who guide the reader through the world in which the text was created. The chosen texts are faithfully transcribed, the biographical and local background explored, and the documents set in historical context. This series will prove invaluable for university and school teachers, providing superb material for essays and textual analysis in class. Above all, it offers a novel opportunity for readers interested in Irish history to discover fresh and exciting sources of personal testimony.

Other titles in the series:

Forthcoming titles:

David Fitzpatrick teaches history at Trinity College, Dublin. His books include *Politics and Irish Life, 1913–1921* (1977, reissued 1998) and *Oceans of Consolation: Personal Accounts of Irish Migration to Australia* (1995).

The Reynolds Letters
An Irish Emigrant Family in
Late Victorian Manchester

Edited by
Lawrence W. McBride

CORK UNIVERSITY PRESS

First published in 1999 by
Cork University Press
Cork
Ireland

© Cork University Press 1999

British Library Cataloguing in Publication Data

A CIP catalogue record for this book is available from the British Library.

ISBN 1 85918 200 3

Typesetting by Red Barn Publishing, Skeagh, Skibbereen

Printed in Ireland by ColourBooks, Baldoyle, Co. Dublin

Contents

Acknowledgements

Family and local histories usually examine small topics, limiting their scope to a few people, a specific place, and a short period of time. The historian must be able to show where his or her analysis of that sampling of people, space and time intersects with the general interpretations that have been reached previously by specialists in the field. At their best, family and local histories illuminate history's fundamental themes, including its patterns of social and political interaction, aspects of cultural diffusion and human interaction with the environment, as well as the role of values, beliefs and ideals in shaping the actions of people in the past. If I have achieved any success in shedding light on the history of Manchester's Irish emigrant population between 1849 and 1904, a large share of the credit must go to others.

My first debt is owed to the *Irish Narratives* series editor, Professor David Fitzpatrick, and to his associates who produce this series at Cork University Press. Professor Fitzpatrick saw the potential merit in the Reynolds letters and encouraged me to follow through to the completion of the project. Raymond Gillespie, Professor of Modern History at the National University of Ireland at Maynooth, pointed me towards the sources on Irish local history, and Patrick Scanlon at the General Valuation Office in Dublin guided me to the records under his purview. Other local sources were searched at the National Archives in Dublin. The Most Rev. Colm O'Reilly, Bishop of Ardagh and Clanmacnoise, granted me permission to review the parish records for Mohill, County Leitrim, at the National Library of Ireland in Dublin. Seán Ó Súilleabháin, County Librarian in Ballinamore, County Leitrim, and Ruth-Ann Harris in Boston were kind enough to correspond with me about circumstances surrounding smallholders who emigrated from Mohill during the Famine. Several research institutions in Manchester and Salford gave me access to their collections: Manchester Central Library, both its Archives and Local History Unit sections, where I was assisted by Mr David Taylor; the John Rylands Library; the Manchester and Lancashire

Acknowledgements

Family History Society at Clayton House; the Greater Manchester
County Record Office; and Chetham's Library. In Salford I visited the
Working Class Movement Library and the Salford Local History
Library. Father David Lannon assisted me at the Salford Diocesian
Archives in Burnley. I owe special thanks to Mervyn Busteed, Professor of Geography at the University of Manchester, who provided me
with both encouragement and direction in his adopted city. Professor
Emmet Larkin and Professor Gary Owens provided helpful criticism of
an early draft of the Introduction. Mrs Sandra Kidwell helped prepare
the manuscript for publication. My research was facilitated by a grant
from Illinois State University.

Nothing at all would have been possible if the Reynolds manuscripts
had not been carefully preserved by family members in Chicago over
the last sixty-five years. The collection has been handed down to me by
my mother, Anita Reynolds McBride, who obtained them from her
father, William Patrick Reynolds, who in turn had received them from
his sister, Mary. Both my mother and my father, Lawrence J. McBride,
have been excellent keepers of the family's oral history and helped me
identify the large cast of the characters in the correspondence. This
excursion into family and emigrant history probably came as a big sur-
prise to my wife, Sandra, who has watched me go off to Ireland over
the past few summers to work on an altogether different project. Now
I have come back with this. For her forbearance and more, this book is
dedicated to her.

Introduction

In October 1934 James William Reynolds of Chicago, Illinois, arrived in Manchester, England, to settle the estate of his late uncle, William Reynolds. James was the logical choice among family members to conduct this legal business. He was a retired accountant and had been to Manchester once before, when, as a young man, he had worked in his uncle's dyeing and dry-cleaning works. As he organised his uncle's belongings, James found a box filled with old documents. Carefully examining the contents, he was surprised to discover some letters from Chicago that William and his mother and sister had received from James's father, Laurence, who was William's older brother. James described the discovery in a brief letter home to his sister, unaware that she had saved an even larger number of family letters that had been sent from Manchester to Laurence's family in Chicago. After he had discharged his responsibilities James brought the documents back to Chicago, where both sides of the correspondence were joined. The complete collection includes over 300 letters and spans a period of nearly seventy years: the earliest surviving letter was received in 1866; the last one was posted in 1934.

The letters presented here are a generous selection from those written between 1877 and 1904. The early letters were written principally by William's mother, Mary Reynolds, who dictated the contents either to her only daughter, Mary Ann, or to William. Mary Ann and William also wrote many letters to Laurence's family over their own signatures. Collectively the correspondence tells the story of a family from Mohill, County Leitrim, that emigrated to Manchester during the Great Famine. The experiences of emigrant families such as the Reynoldses have interested many historians, and the Irish in Manchester and the contiguous city of Salford have attracted particular attention. Early studies from the middle of the nineteenth century describe an emigrant Irish population that lived in hopeless poverty.[1] Those dark interpretations influenced the popular perception of the Manchester Irish for many years, and historians have only recently begun to suggest that the city's Irish citizens contributed far more to its economic and social development than unskilled and casual labour.[2] One problem facing historians of Irish emigrant life generally, however, has been the lack of contemporary accounts of Irish people speaking directly to other Irish people. Diaries, letters and photographs provide insights into popular attitudes concerning such phenomena as social mobility and class-consciousness, yet too few individuals recorded information about them as they were happening.[3] The accounts contained in the Reynoldses' letters help fill that gap in our understanding. The letters illuminate the mental and social world of a successful emigrant family, busily attaining respectability and making money as dry cleaners, silk dyers and shopkeepers in the industrial city that acquired worldwide notoriety because its Irish population lived in the most squalid conditions in Europe.

The Reynolds story began about 1830 when Patrick Reynolds, from the barony and parish of Mohill and the townland of Carrick in County Leitrim, married Mary O'Toole, whose family lived about two miles to the west in the parish of Annaduff in a townland also called Carrick (both townlands were sometimes spelled 'Corrick'). They established a home in Patrick's townland and had a fruitful marriage. Of nine children, six survived childhood: Laurence, John, Peter, Mary Ann, Patrick, and the youngest, William, who was baptised on 26 May 1847.[4] Carrick was on Sir Morgan George Crofton's estate and was one of Leitrim's smaller townlands, containing a mere fifty acres of arable and pasture land out of a total of eighty-two acres. The Tithe Composition Book for the Parish of Mohill (1834), which was used to set the amount of tithe paid to the established Church of Ireland, indicates that a Thomas Reynolds (Patrick's father was named Laurence) had the largest holding: it included quality arable and pasture land totalling over thirty-one acres.[5] Upon Thomas's death, the land was divided among Patrick (who held two of the townland's seven arable lots) and James, John and Charles Reynolds and Abel O'Donnell and Bryan Reilly. Patrick paid a reasonable rent of £2 18s on each of his holdings, which were each valued at £3 5s.[6] The Ordnance Survey map shows Patrick's and the other tenants' houses and outbuildings clustered in a clachan near a five-acre lake.[7] Working within the traditional rundale agricultural system, the families probably planted oats, turnips and some potatoes. Pigs, butter and eggs were sold to local jobbers in the busy market town of Mohill for export via Longford town to England.[8] It is likely that the older children attended one of Mohill's two national schools, where they would have learned to read and write.[9]

Patrick Reynolds died on 13 January 1849 at the age of thirty-nine.[10] It is not known if his death was related to the Famine, although Mohill was especially hard hit by the catastrophe. He was survived by his thirty-eight-year-old widow and six children. According to Reynolds family oral tradition, Mary left Mohill with the children within a few months of her husband's death and emigrated to Manchester. One can only speculate as to how she financed the journey across Ireland and the subsequent passage to England, but it is likely that Mary's experience was similar to that of thousands of other Famine emigrants. She might have had some money saved, or members of the Reynolds or O'Toole families who remained in Carrick and nearby townlands might have provided assistance. Her older sons might have worked along the way in exchange for ground transport and the steamer fare, which ranged from 2s to 5s per person.[11] While there is no record of the disposition of her holding, Griffith's Valuation of Rateable Property (1857) and the Revision Books in the General Valuation Office (dating from 1860) indicate that one of her lots passed to a Patrick Reynolds, whose relationship to Mary is not clear, and the other eventually passed to Patrick junior.[12] One can only speculate, moreover, about her route. In the years before the Famine migrant Irish workers followed an established route from Leitrim to the ports of Drogheda and Dublin and from there crossed the Irish Sea to Liverpool, the debarkation point for thousands of Irish emigrants during the Famine.[13] Again, according to family oral history, Mary and her children walked some thirty miles along the towpaths of the waterways connecting Liverpool to Manchester. As for the choice of Manchester as her destination, aside from the attraction of employment in its burgeoning cotton mills, the 1851 census returns reveal that there were many families and individuals named Reynolds already living in the city, but there is no evidence in either the correspondence or oral history that Mary relied on other Reynolds families in any process of chain migration.[14]

The experiences of the family after 1850 can be partially reconstructed by combining information in the letters with data found in other documents. The family does not appear in the 1851 census returns for either Manchester or Salford.[15] The 1861 census, however, shows Mary Reynolds and her children residing in Manchester at 8 Buxton Street in the All Saints Ward, Chorlton-upon-Medlock, just across the River Medlock from 'Little Ireland', the slum that gave the city its notorious reputation.[16] As studies of family structure in early nineteenth-century Lancashire have demonstrated, emigrant families often moved their places of residence, but they did not move very far.[17] Assuming that the Reynoldses lived at, or in close proximity to, their Buxton Street address from the time they arrived in Manchester, one can conclude that their transition from rural to urban life must have been shocking. The tremendous influx of Irish emigrants caused Manchester's population to swell from 243,000 in 1841 to over 300,000 in 1851 and placed incredible stress on the city's housing and amenities. The environment of All Saints Ward and the six adjacent wards where the Irish congregated was the subject of a series of street-by-street investigations by visitors from the Manchester and Salford Sanitary Association, founded in 1852 to promote the attention of emigrants to temperance, personal and domestic cleanliness, and to the laws of health generally. Their reports condemned the area's unhealthy back-to-back housing construction, the permanently damp cellars that were unfit for human habitation, the open drains, oozing sewers, overflowing privies, and the filthy piggeries. The Medlock was impeded by carcasses of dead animals and bubbled with noxious gasses. Buxton Street was not the worst place in Chorlton, but it was typical of the surrounding slums: crowded and foul.[18]

Mary Reynolds had ideas about how her family could escape from this squalor. In her letters she consistently emphasised the virtues of hard work and temperance as the keys to success and security. More-over, her younger sons attended the Xaverian Brothers' school nearby in St Augustine's parish on Granby Row, and the careful penmanship in her daughter's letters indicates that she also received some formal edu-cation, perhaps at the same school where the Sisters of Notre Dame taught the girls.[19] By 1861 everyone in the family was at work. The cen-sus return of that year shows that Mary was the head of the household; John worked as a mechanic, Peter was a bayonet grinder, Mary Ann was a machine stitcher, Patrick was a machine turner, and young William worked as an errand boy. Laurence left Buxton Street around 1860 and emigrated to New Jersey. He married Mary Ann Kavanagh from County Dublin, and they moved on to the south side of Chicago, arriv-ing there around 1865.

Notice of other changes that occurred in the family's life during the 1860s is provided in an early and very revealing letter, dated 5 September 1868, from Mary to Laurence. It was sent on the occasion of the birth of his first child, James William, who was born earlier that year. (Laurence told his mother that he named the new arrival after his brother William. When his mother and brother expressed their delight with the choice of the name, Laurence and his wife continued to refer to James as William for nearly fifteen years!) Mary began the letter by expressing her happiness that Laurence and his family were all in good health. She wrote: 'I Hope God will prosper your son, that he may live to be a Big man.' Commenting on the photographs Laurence had sent to her, she observed: 'Your Mrs Looks well But yourself Looks thin. I think it must Be from the Heat of the weather. We Have had a very warm summer here, the Hottest it has Been for meny years.' Later in the letter she again expressed concern over his appearance, noting that a friend who had also viewed the photograph thought he was looking thin; the friend remarked that Laurence's 'hens must give him some fresh eggs to eat'. A deeper reason for Mary's concern over her son's health becomes evident in another part of the letter that related news of his brother Peter. She explained that his health was precarious and that his journeys between Manchester and the seaside near Dublin in an attempt to recover his strength had not had the desired effect. She reported further that Peter had returned to Ireland with his wife and an infant daughter to try to restore his health and launch a business in Carrick-on-Shannon as a butter and egg buyer. Peter was, in fact, abandoning a successful business in Manchester; since 1865 he had operated a greengrocery and beer-retailing business at 20 Brook Street in Chorlton. An index of both his success and her concern was Mary's report that 'he Sold his House Cart and Horse and part of his furniture to John for £11 0 shillings. He sold them for far less than he would get from the stranger.' She then added: 'He took Home with him a Bout £130. John owes Him a Bout £20 more and a Bout £20 more that He is promised from his Depters. If He Had His Health this 2 years He Could Have Brought meny a Hundreth more with Him onley for Dr Bills and Going from one Seaport to another and His childer Dyeing.' Next Mary gave Laurence news of his other brothers and his sister. John, who had taken over Peter's shop, had 'Left his work all together and He is shureto Do well if he keeps Sober. He Has no troble or Care But to mind his Busness. Patrick Left his work to go and Live with Him Because He Had a knowladge of the Busness . . . William works at Wrights still.[20] Maryan is working at her old place.' She also forwarded the latest news that Peter had sent from Annaduff: 'Unkel William hed a very good Crop that he hed as much potatos that would Do him for 12 months if thare Comes no rot over tham.' Her own health was 'but middling. Peter going away has Brote a great Deal off Sorrow on me But I hope with the help of God i will Be able to go and see him. He said whan he was going as soon as he would get Settled he would send for me Because it was a great Loss to part with him. Many a pound he gave me since you went away. May God restore his health.'

This letter indicates that Mary Reynolds's family still lacked a stable aggregate income that would permit it to survive a severe financial crisis. While Mary and her children had moved beyond the mere subsistence level, they had not yet reached the financial equilibrium that was critical for working-class people who hoped to make further economic advances.[21]

But things were improving. The family moved from Buxton Street to 31 Gibson Street, Ardwick, near the site of the famous rescue in 1867 of two Fenian prisoners from a police van by a party of their comrades.[22] A letter to Chicago, dated 30 October 1870, provided further news. Mary opened this letter by thanking Laurence for sending her £9, an indication that he was doing quite well in Chicago and that he had taken the earlier hint from his mother about Peter's generosity to her. Her letter also provides an additional explanation for Laurence's generosity. She stated that the alarming news she had sent to him in her most recent letter was an awful mistake: Patrick was not, as had been reported to her, killed in an accident. He was, however, seriously injured and had been under a doctor's care for three weeks. His sister Mary Ann, moreover, had also been under a doctor's care for three weeks and was only now beginning to recover. Patrick, she then reported, had returned to his work at the lathe, but 'there is no poorer work in the world working at 15 shillings per week'. On a brighter note, she wrote: 'William cant Complain of his work. His wages is very tiday. He is getting 26 shillings per week now. Only for his wages wee would not be able to keep our House.' 'Whenever he makes any over time', she added, he 'gets 6½d an hour for it. If Patrick had luck to have constant work wee would be pretty well.' She also asked if Laurence had any news of her brother John, who had emigrated from Carrick to Shullsburg, Lafayette County, Wisconsin, but who was not much of a correspondent. She hoped that the recent arrival of his wife would make him more communicative. Mary explained in another letter some years later that her mother left an obligation on her father to look after John above all the other children, and that burden had apparently fallen on her. Noting that John would now be fifty-three years of age, she wrote: 'We wood be all wishful to heare from him and i wood like to corrispond with him myself Before i dye and see his likeness.' In time Mary learned from Laurence that her brother had become a prosperous farmer with several fine sons and daughters and 200 acres of splendid land, cattle and horses. Over the next thirty years members of Laurence's and John O'Toole's families exchanged letters and visits, but

John seldom wrote to his sister; indeed, three years passed between one of his letters and the next.

As these early letters and other supporting evidence indicate, the Reynoldses had a precarious existence between 1850 and 1870. Their experience supports the conclusions of recent research on urban nuclear families in Lancashire during this period: they were subjected to severe pressures that affected relationships between parents and their children and also among the children.[23] Some families were shattered; other devised mechanisms that not only helped them cope with life in a hostile environment but also pulled them closer together. Mary Reynolds and her children experienced both pressures. Her eldest son, Laurence, was gone, never to return. She took some comfort as his family continued to grow. In addition to James (still referred to in the letters as William until one of John O'Toole's daughters innocently referred to him by his correct name, causing some understandable confusion in Manchester), there were six other children, two of whom died in childhood. Laurence was employed in the Chicago and Rock Island Rail Road machine shop, grinding the spikes that held the tracks in place — work that was poorly paid and dirty. During the 1880s and 1890s Laurence tried other occupations, but was periodically out of work. In her letters to him Mary frequently encouraged him to set up a business and to see to it that young James went to work, advice that annoyed Laurence and his wife, who did not appreciate this long-distance interference in their lives.[24] Meanwhile Peter's health continued to fail, and he died in Ireland some time between 1871 and 1877. The fate of his family is unknown. John was the next of her sons to leave and marry. He and his wife, Bridget, were childless. He eventually became the proprietor of two greengroceries: the old Reynolds shop on Brook Street and one on Travis Street, Hulme, where he and his wife lived. John also purchased some residential properties; his wife collected the rents.

Meanwhile the youngest children, Mary Ann, Patrick and William, lived with and supported their ageing mother, who continued to be identified as the head of the household until the 1891 census. This designation was both an indication that she continued to accept her responsibilities as their mother and a mark of her children's respect for her. They did not marry. The letters Mary and her remaining children sent to Chicago after 1877 provide a candid account of how they prospered beyond anything they could have imagined only a few years earlier. Mary proved to be an accurate chronicler of the life and times of her family. Her letters included information about health, the weather, employment, strikes, news of family members' comings and goings, as well as reports of and reactions to events in Ireland and England. More than anything else, however, her letters, as well as those of Mary Ann and William, tell the story of her youngest son's developing entrepreneurial skills and spirit.

Mary was correct when she wrote that William was making a 'tiday' wage; his overtime wages were a significant addition to the family purse. Recent research indicates that in 1871 wages for the best-paid men in Lancashire's dyeworks (workers who were known as 'slabs' or 'slubbers' after the stray pieces of wool found in finished pieces of cloth) were £1 4s for sixty hours, with the rest of the labour force receiving between 18s and £1 2s. In busy periods it was common for labourers to work in excess of ninety hours per week without additional overtime pay.[25] By 1873 William had gained sufficient knowledge of his trade at George Wright & Sons — there was no formal apprenticeship until much later — to open his own shop at 23 Bedford Street in Chorlton. Although Mary's letters and other family documents do not reveal anything about the sources of William's risk capital, he probably used his savings and the money his mother had received from Laurence and Peter as well as money earned by Mary Ann and Patrick to establish himself in business. He saved some labour costs and was able to devote his time to other aspects of the business because his mother, sister and brother worked with him. Mary Ann's experience as a worker in the garment industry was a bonus. His mother also contributed by operating a collection point at their home where customers could drop off their clothing, thereby saving William the cost of hiring an agent to do this work. Patrick spared William the necessary heavy work. Because William never married, the time and money that might have gone into supporting a family were diverted into the shop. It was, in any case, dangerous work. Accidents were frequent, including limbs crushed by machinery and injuries caused by falls into kiers full of boiling water or caustic dyes.[26] His sister recalled in a letter some twenty years later that William worked in the shop's cramped cellar for six years, with only a two-inch crack in the flagstones above to allow the steam to escape.

Working together in the fledgling enterprise, the Reynoldses entered into a basic bargain of economic interdependence that augmented their bonds of affection and loyalty — and helped them prosper. Within two years Mary and her remaining children moved again, this time to a larger house at 281 Regents Road on the outskirts of Salford, away from the crowded slums in that city. In a letter to Laurence dated 2 July 1877 Mary wrote: 'My health is pretty good at present. I take some sleeping drops for My sleep and I do not think it injers my health.' She then observed casually that the family was 'going on as yousal. Williams work is not so busy at present. He imploys 3 a man woman and boy. He is not doing much himself. His health is not so very good.' She then added that the 'work is very hard and he worked hard when he first commenced so he wants to give himself more rest than he did in the beginning'. Things continued to improve. In the autumn of 1878 William opened the second shop in what would become over the next fifteen years a large network of collection points, shops and works across Manchester and Salford. When trade was slack, as it often was during the summer or during unexpected economic downturns, William's business still turned a profit. As Mary wrote to Laurence on 11 June 1883, explaining that she did not expect him to repay the money she had recently sent to him, 'I have More Money in the bank than I will Ever be able to Spend. We have all of us got a plentiness of Money, thanks be to god for all his blessings to us. We ware very fortunite Since William comenced in buisness. Every thing Seemed to prosper with us for we are under very heavy Expenses. Still the Money Keeps coming in.' The Reynoldses now enjoyed a steady financial surplus. Mary and her children were able to send money regularly to Chicago — first £2, then £5, with smaller amounts and gifts enclosed for the children at Christmas and Easter. Money and clothing was also sent back to Ireland in response to periodic requests from relatives in Mohill.

William plowed the profits from his operation back into the business, purchasing new machinery and horses for transport and advertising his services. His records from 1885/6 indicate that he protected his investments by purchasing insurance policies, always looking for lower premiums and expanded coverage. William, Mary Ann and Patrick routinely worked longer hours than the employees, and William watched his workers' performance like a hawk. In typical business fashion, he complained about taxes, competition and indebtedness. He was especially concerned about the cost of food and coal prices in Manchester, which affected how much his customers could afford to spend on cleaning and the overhead cost of his fuel and coal-based cleaning fluids. Ultimately he benefited by developments in the dyeing industry, which after 1870 was rapidly becoming a profession, as evidenced by the formation of organisations and advisory boards that shared information and ideas. The finely produced *Dyer, Calico Printer, Bleacher, Finisher, and Textile Review,* for example, published market prices in England and abroad and also provided regular features on international trade, dyeing patterns, chemical recipes, technological innovations, legal cases, book reviews, and more.[27]

In July 1892 a fire destroyed the works where William processed his customers' goods; his landlord was under-insured and would not rebuild. William wrote to his brother in Chicago explaining the situation: 'The amount of work we had to do was Something enormous. For myself I can Say I passed through the most trying time of my life and Just Managed to pull through with the narrowest escape of loosing our business.' In fact William rebounded stronger than ever. He borrowed money to purchase new machinery and the old Spring Bank mill with adjacent properties off Stockport Road on Chell Street and Brook Terrace in Longsight. He refitted the mill for his dyeworks, which he

claimed was one of the largest in England. He also diversified his holdings, purchasing property in Hulme that included houses, shops and
stables. His modest stock portfolio included shares in several banks,
investment trusts and corporations. He eventually purchased more
property adjacent to his works and opened a laundry that helped him
secure the trade of the city's major hotels. William also developed a
niche market: cleaning the finest silk fabric.

By the 1890s the Reynoldses had come to typify Manchester's
upwardly mobile Irish emigrant families who were seeking and finding
middle-class respectability. Now well beyond the challenge of balanc-
ing income and expenditure to make ends meet, families like the
Reynoldses were anxious to enjoy the social benefits that accompanied
economic prosperity, although in their intensely competitive world,
position and status had constantly to be reasserted.[28] When Laurence's
son James arrived from Chicago in June 1894 to learn sound business
practices from his uncle William, he wrote home reporting: 'They have
a very fine home, out of sight, you bet. There is not many of your upper
ten people got a home like it, fine furniture, also a fine piano. Everything is tiptop style. I have a room to myself. There is a bathroom too.'
A few days later he elaborated: 'The window of my room overlooks
Old Trafford Park, a very pretty spot which is surrounded by some of
the prettiest houses in Manchester. I tell you the Reynolds are top
notchers here. Sit in the front seat in church. Wears a nobby silk tie.
Right in line, that's uncle William.' The results of the upward economic
and social trajectory that James captured in his letters can be traced
geographically through the changes in the family's addresses. From
Chorlton and Ardwick to Salford's Regents Road, they moved on to
larger, better-appointed homes back in Manchester, first at 295 Stretford Road, and then to 1 Dudley Place in Old Trafford. From there
they moved to 3 Clarence Road, Longsight, on the edge of Victoria
Park, the most exclusive area in the city. But William wanted to reside
on the edge of the city, where the air was fresher and the larger lots
would allow his mother to do a bit of gardening. The family's next
move, therefore, was to 1 Norton Place, Wilmslow Road, Fallowfield;

and finally, in 1904, to 293 Wilmslow Road. This path was typical of members of Manchester's business elite. The distance away from one's place of business was proportionate to their success: the further away, yet still within easy reach in case of an emergency, the better.

The letters and other family documents reveal much about what the family members thought was important. Mary Ann and William urged Laurence to see to it that their nephews and niece in Chicago attended to their education, and they emphasised the importance of prayer, as exemplified by their mother's piety. The family also stayed in close contact with their relatives and family friends in Ireland. In the autumn of 1878 Mary returned to Mohill, where she found everyone in good form. She made a final visit with William, Patrick, and Mary Ann in 1883, and the children made annual holiday visits to Annaduff and Carrick and other townlands near Mohill for many years. The Bray Head Hotel in County Wicklow was one of their favourite places. William also took holiday trips to France. In 1896 Mary Ann crossed the Atlantic to visit Laurence's family in Chicago, the O'Tooles in Wisconsin, and other cousins in New York.

The letters from Manchester also convey some of the negative connotations one attaches to the *nouveau riche*. For example, although the family's economic fortunes continually improved, Mary Ann, who had nearly £1,000 in her bank account in 1900, hated to pay a few pennies postage due on letters from America. When she sent fine gifts to Chicago, she explained in advance letters that she had ticked the 'used goods' box on the envelope in order to save the customs duty. After sending gifts, the Reynoldses always looked expectantly for gracious letters of thanks, and they did not hesitate to complain if they thought the thanks received were insufficient. But they were not parsimonious. When it was time to purchase a new vehicle, William imported an expensive van from the Reynoldses' coachbuilders in Mohill. When a family member was ill, they did not hesitate to call in doctors and nurses to attend to their needs. And when they took their meals, they knew how to enjoy themselves. Holiday meals were especially bountiful: turkey and all the trimmings, vegetables, sweets, Bass ale, champagne, other wines, and Jameson's whiskey. Photographs show William and his sister wearing beautifully tailored clothes. William's neighbours referred to him as 'the Lord of Fallowfield' on account of his smart appearance.

Their home in Fallowfield was equally well appointed. There was artwork everywhere: in the dining-room a picture entitled 'Mary Magdalene Anointing Our Lord's Feet' and engravings entitled 'Daniel O'Connell', 'The Village Politician', 'The Blind Fiddler' and 'The Piper'; in the hall a small picture of 'The Madonna and Child'; and in the drawing-room another 'Madonna and Child'. William was good at recitations and had an excellent singing voice, although no one could play the piano. The large mahogany bookcase was filled with papers and books, including the family Bible, old school books and a *de luxe* edition of Moore's *Irish Melodies*. Bedside tables held photo cabinets of the scattered family members and religious objects. Everything was kept in order by a live-in maid and William's man-servant.

John Reynolds and his wife, although successful in their shops and real estate holdings, seemed to be less concerned than Mary Ann and William with keeping up appearances. Although letters to Laurence usually indicated that 'John and wife is well and doing well', a rift had developed between John and his siblings. Things came to a head in March 1895 when John and his wife refused to ride in a carriage with William and Mary Ann at their mother's funeral; John also refused to help defray the cost of the funeral and burial.

There was also a psychologically unsettling aspect to working tirelessly to attain economic success and maintain social standing in a foreign land. The Reynoldses understood that, as Irish emigrants, they could never find complete acceptance in England. Writing on 16 November 1884 to his young cousin Bridget, who had inquired from Mohill about emigrating to Manchester, William extended two warnings. First he explained: 'You would never be happy again once you left Ireland. Let me advise you thare is no place like the old country.' He then added: 'To come to this wicked country you would have all up hill work to do. Thare are plenty of our country people in Manchester [who] never raised thamselves but are in a state now as they were 30 years ago. I had a slise of good Luck because I started in Business on my own acount. Only for that I would be working from Day to Day for Small Screw and never have anything and never be able to visit the old Land.'

His concern for his relatives was shared by all the family members and was revealed by the affection they expressed for loved ones who were separated by vast distances, as well as by the emotions released when there were illnesses or deaths in the family. Mary's letters frequently included tender passages that she intended would be read out to her grandchildren, reminding them to say their prayers, help their parents, and stay away from troublemakers. The physical separation and time between communications made the writers impatient when a letter failed to supply full details on everyone's doings. In the final analysis, however, Mary was as quick to forgive as she was to chastise. On 24 March 1884 she replied to Laurence's last and too brief letter: 'We thought your letter rather cold. You never mentioned Mary Ann or the children in it. You know that we always like to hear how they are as long as you had plenty of paper left. We will excuse you this time on account of the cold weather. It is not so pleasant to rite.' She missed her son, and her children missed each other. In a short letter some twenty-five years after his departure, Mary wrote: 'Dear Laurence, it was on this day of the Month that you Left us 4th of Feb. It seems a Long Time.'

The family's religious faith was an important source of spiritual solace in the face of separation from family members. The Reynoldses were longstanding members of St Wilfrid's Catholic parish, Hulme, an area with a large working-class Irish emigrant population; they joined St Cuthbert's parish when they moved to Fallowfield. Mary attended mass daily at nearby chapels until her health declined, and William and Mary Ann made visits to St Joseph's church on their way to the works in Longsight. Their Catholicism and their ethnicity were vitally important to them and, as was the case of Irish emigrants in Manchester generally, were inextricably linked. As the number of native-born Irish people declined in Manchester during the last quarter of the nineteenth century, membership of St Wilfrid's provided them with a sense of continuity with an earlier period and the people they knew. The Reynoldses entertained their respective parish priests in their homes and befriended Manchester's most respected priest, St Wilfrid's Very Rev. Canon Patrick Laurence O'Toole, who naturally took a great interest in them when writing his massive *History of the Clan O'Toole* (1890).[29] The family received several Catholic newspapers from America, and they were critical of periodicals that expressed any hostility to their faith or nation.

All three letter-writers commented on the prejudice that the English people directed towards the Irish, but their letters also reveal that the Reynoldses never felt any special loyalty or obligation to England. When they wrote to Laurence about 'the state of the country', they were referring to events in Ireland, not England. They were, for example, far more interested in the city's Jubilee Trade Exhibition in 1887 and the opening of the Manchester Ship Canal in 1894 than they were in Queen Victoria's visit to the city that year or in her Diamond Jubilee in 1897. Mary Reynolds was blunt about the English, as symbolised by the queen. She wrote to Laurence in June 1882: 'We can Do vary well without royalty in Ireland. The[y] never Done anything for Ireland but punis the people and Make Emigrants of them.' Letters written during the South African War showed a cool disinterest in British losses; the rise in coal prices and the increase in taxes to pay for the war mattered more to William and his sister. Sometimes, however, the Reynoldses' upward economic mobility clashed with their ethnicity and former class loyalties. Mary, Mary Ann and William had no sympathy for the fate of Irish landlords during the Land War, and while they were always interested in news about strikes, they disliked any English and Irish labourers who proved to be unreliable or untrustworthy. Mary believed working men spent too much time drinking in public houses and were, therefore, responsible for their own problems; William believed increased wages and shorter working hours diminished profits, ultimately forcing employers to lay off workers.

Manchester's and Salford's political life reinforced the sense of ethnicity among the Irish population, linking Irish people of all classes in a common cause.[30] Loyal supporters of Charles Stewart Parnell and the Irish Parliamentary Party during the 1880s, the two branches of the Reynolds family kept one another abreast of the sensational events in the Land War and the struggle for Home Rule for Ireland. On 8 December 1880 Mary Ann expressed the family's continuing faith and hope: 'We have meeting about ireland. It is all the talk of the Day. We Spend all the Spare time we Have Reading the papers we get from ireland. If the people all Stick up to Mr Parnell the[y] will get SomeThing Done at last for poor Old Ireland.' Newspapers carrying Irish political news were exchanged between Chicago and Manchester, and Laurence reported on Parnell's and other Irish Party fund-raisers' speeches to Chicago's Irish audiences. The early 1880s were tense times for Irish nationalist activists around Manchester. Rumours of potential Fenian outrages filled both the Liberal *Salford Weekly News* and the Conservative *Manchester Evening News*, and a serious explosion in the Salford barracks in January 1881 seemed to confirm the worst fears. The John Dillon Branch of the Irish National Land League in Salford was careful not to leave any records that could be used in a trial, should the branch be suppressed and its leaders prosecuted. Mary Ann and William were active in that branch, and in January 1882 they both sat on the platform when Anna Parnell, the sister of the Irish nationalist leader, spoke to 4,000 people in the Free Trade Hall in Manchester. They no doubt also supported the John Dillon Branch's expression of indignation at the assassination of the Chief Secretary for Ireland, Lord Frederick Cavendish, and his Under-Secretary, T. H. Burke, in the Phoenix Park, Dublin, in May 1882.

Irish emigrants were also deeply interested in English political affairs. Families such as the Reynoldses had to pay particular attention to public policies that affected their economic and social position. Irish votes for Liberal supporters of Home Rule, moreover, could tip the balance in the closely fought municipal and national elections in both Manchester and Salford.[31] William and John, who as householders and business owners had two votes, supported Jacob Bright, the local

Liberal member of parliament, and William sat on the platform at the Liberals' political meetings. One measure of the level of William's political participation was that local politicians asked him to offer himself as a candidate for the local council in Salford's Ordsall district, but he demurred. While co-operation with Home Rulers in the Liberal Party became increasingly important for Irish nationalists after 1886, when the Liberals divided on the issue, the Reynoldses' ultimate political allegiance was to Ireland. As a respectable middle-class Catholic nationalist, William agreed in 1890 with the Catholic bishops that Parnell was not fit to lead the Irish Party after the O'Shea divorce case, but he questioned the propriety of the interference of the Liberal Party leader, William Ewart Gladstone, in the Irish Party's decision that brought their leader down.

William's brother Patrick died in the prime of life in 1889, just as the family business reached one of its high points. His mother died in 1895. Constantly worried about her health, Mary Reynolds had reached the advanced age of eighty-four years. Laurence died in Chicago in 1898. His sister Mary Ann died in 1904 aged fifty-seven. John was next; his shops had previously been taken over by Hughie Reynolds, a nephew from Mohill who had worked earlier for William at the dyeworks, another example of how the family members worked together to help each other prosper. These successive deaths in the immediate family devastated William. From that point on, for nearly thirty years, William lived alone at the house on Wilmslow Road. His correspondence with the Chicago Reynoldses came to a virtual standstill.

Because of the ensuing gap in the correspondence between 1904 and 1921, it is impossible to know how William managed his business interests or how he reacted to some of the central events of that period. The passage of the welfare state legislation between 1906 and 1912, the old age pensions and national health insurance, for example, would have interested him, if only as an employer who paid part of the costs. However, letters to Chicago from Annie Masterson, one of the Reynoldses' cousins in Manchester, provide some information.

William's health was strong, and he continued to work hard at his business. He also continued to travel, visiting Germany, Austria, Sweden and Russia just before the outbreak of the First World War. In a letter written in July 1915 to his nephew James, he blamed Germany for starting the war, which caused inflation and depressed trade. Both situations were bad for his business; naïvely, he thought that the arrival of Irish troops at the front would quickly turn the tide. No letters survive about the 1916 Easter Rising, the rise of Sinn Féin or the War of Independence. During the Civil War William supported the pro-Treaty side that accepted the establishment of the Irish Free State and the partition of the country. On 30 January 1922 he wrote to his youngest nephew, William:

> Ireland is beginning to settle down now with the Irish Free State and we are all looking forward to the time when the country gets settled and there will be good times in store for Ireland. It seems to me that almost every country in Europe is wishful to commence business with Ireland and I think that after a time Ireland will commence to have a prosperous and happy time.

He remained guardedly optimistic throughout the year, explaining to William in a typewritten letter on 12 December:

> I was very sorry to see how things were going on across the water. After all the centuries of persecution that Ireland has passed through. We all think in Manchester that the Free State Bill that passed Parliament is a first class bill for Ireland, almost equal to a Republic, and there is no doubt that if the people of the twenty-six counties all pulled together, and if they wanted they could get a Republic afterwards . . . As I understand, ten Irishmen out of every twelve in England seem to think that there is everything in the bill the people require, and can make use of it in every way to make the country happy and prosperous, as nothing is left out of the bill. The only thing is the connection with the British Empire which will never do any harm to the people of the country when the new state

is established and in first class working order. We do not know how
the country will come on at present, but we all hope for the best.

These letters were among the first of a series of exchanges between
Uncle William, as he came to be called, and his namesake. Throughout
the 1920s the ageing uncle transmitted advice and encouragement to
the young businessman from Chicago. As always, he sought American
newspapers with sound Catholic and Irish views, and young William
eagerly obliged. William was pleased when his nephew's family began
to grow, complimenting him on the pictures of the baby girls and the
son that he received in the mail. Meanwhile William's and James's sister, Mary, visited her uncle in Manchester, and she travelled on to Ireland with her cousin, Anne Masterson, thereby establishing a
relationship between the second generation of the Reynoldses'
extended families.

William Reynolds continued to travel and manage his business
throughout the 1920s. In 1924 he joined a group of pilgrims from Manchester — including Cardinal Francis Bourne, three bishops, nearly
forty priests, and one hundred others — who visited the Holy Land.
The group met Pope Pius XI in Rome on their return trip. After the
six-week tour William wrote to a friend declaring that shaking hands
with the pope and kissing his ring was 'the greatest pleasure and priv-
iledge of my life'. His travelling companion, Canon James Rowntree,
parish priest at St Cuthbert's, was his closest friend during these years.
William demonstrated his gratitude to the priest by subscribing £700
towards the construction of a new high altar in the church.

By 1930 William's pace began to slow. He turned over the day-to-
day operations of the business to a manager, but he lost money every
year during the depression. Meanwhile he put his private financial
affairs in order, arranging for generous gifts totalling some £20,000 for
his nephews and nieces in Chicago and Wisconsin and for the Masterson cousins in Manchester, as well as for his long-serving employees,
housekeepers and servants. He also provided for gifts to his former and
current parishes and their priests, the Xaverian Brothers, the Sisters of

the Poor, the Sisters of St Vincent de Paul, the New and Poor Mission Fund, the Royal Infirmary, and St Bede's College. Proud of his trade, William always referred to himself as a dyer, and was identified as such in his will and in the probate records. He died in his sleep on 8 October 1934 at the age of eighty-four. He was buried in the family plot in the cemetery in Moston Lane, finally at rest with his mother, sister and brother Patrick, under a marble stone which he had purchased on his trip to Italy.

James Reynolds returned to Manchester and liquidated the business and sold off the properties, effectively ending the story of Mary Reynolds and her family in Manchester. Back in America, his sister used her share of the inheritance to purchase seven acres of wooded land on the shore of Lake Michigan in Wisconsin, where she built a fine retirement home for herself and her brothers. She named the place 'Mohill' after the Reynoldses' ancestral home. It remains in the family.

Editorial Note

The selection of emigrant letters presented here has three principal authors: Mary Reynolds, her daughter Mary Ann, and her son William. The early letters in the collection were written in Mary Reynolds's 'voice', but the orthography and penmanship make it clear that Mary dictated the words or ideas to her son or daughter who then drafted the texts, closing them with the collective 'Your Affectionate Mother, Brothers and Sister'. William and Mary Ann also wrote many letters in their own right.

The majority of the letters do not include punctuation marks. The authors' spelling was based largely on the way the words sounded: for example, the spellings *right / wright / write / rite* and *their / there / thare* and *here / hear* are used interchangeably. The phonetic values of some letters of the alphabet have frequently been misunderstood: for example, *sell* is written for *cell*, and *gust* for *just*. In addition, both Mary Ann and

William were inconsistent in their use of capital letters in words that began sentences. Many of their sentences began with lower case characters. Conversely, the authors often employed initial capital letters in words placed elsewhere in a sentence, although they formed smaller, lower case versions of these letters within words. The letters *h*, *k*, *l*, *d*, *s* and *v* at the beginning of a word nearly always rose above the height of other characters on a line. Sometimes these capital letters were used to give added emphasis to a word or phrase, but this usage appears to be more an habitual way of forming the letters. The Reynoldses usually wrote their letters on standard 4in. × 7in. stationery and each page was filled to capacity. Closings were done with a flourish, space permitting. The majority of the writing idiosyncrasies appearing in the letters do not pose any great difficulty for the modern reader.

I have, therefore, attempted to maintain the integrity of the handwritten texts in both the excerpts that appear in the introductory essay and in the texts of the letters that follow. I have not corrected the authors' spelling or grammar, although I have included some obviously missing letters and words within square brackets. Occasional explanatory interpolations or clarifications of obscurities are also given within square brackets.

I have retained the authors' use of initial capital letters wherever they occur, even when it seems that they were not making an emphatic point. In order to facilitate reading, I have throughout imposed a capital letter to indicate the start of a new sentence; I have also supplied full stops wherever they are missing at the conclusion of sentences, and have occasionally supplied other punctuation where the meaning of a sentence might otherwise be in doubt. I have retained all the original paragraphing, only rarely finding it necessary to subdivide some long passages of continuous text by additonal paragraph breaks. Finally, the places and dates, salutations and closings of the letters have been presented in a standardised format.

Letters of the Reynolds Family

Manchester, 1877–1904

281 Regent Road
Manchester
Sep 4th/77

Dear Laurence and Mary Ann,

I recived your Letter and we ware very glad to hear that you ware all well after the great turn out and we ware glad to heare that you did not loose much time in your woork.[1] The papers gave a very Bad acount about it.

Dear Laurence, We are all in prety good health at presant, thanks be to god. If I never witnesed a sason like this for Rains. It is Raining this 9 months without one week Drie. We thought when the harvest wood com it wood be Dry but the month of August we had not a Dry Day in it. The crops are comeplaitly spoiled. I am afraide we will have a hard winter in England.

We are all Doing Prety well. We wood Do Beter onley for the weather. Fine weather is mor Suitable for Williams work.

John is Doing well in his shop. The wether dose not inge [*injure*] his Busness.

Dear Laurence, we ware very glad to hear that William is a good Boy and helps his Mother sow well and I hope he will not forget his granmother and Pray for her and i hope that Johney will Be a good Boy and Pray for his granney and when Thomas and Birnard groes up the[y] will be good Boys.

When we Posted this Letter we Posted one to your uncle John and whither he Answers it or not we Canot tell.

We Will Conclude By Sending oure Love to you all

Laurence and
Mary Ann
William
John and
Thomas
Birnard

I Remane your
Afectionate Mother
til Death

2. Mary Reynolds to Laurence and Mary Ann Reynolds

Manchester
Feb 18/78

Dear Laurence and Mary Ann,

When we Recived you[r] Letter we ware glad to hear that you ware all well and in good health as this leaves us in at Pressant, Thanks be to god fo[r] all his blessings to yus [*us*]. We never neglected your Letter so Long befor. We ware Busey with the new place that William has taken, going Backwards and forwards. He did not understand it properley. When he had taken it he thought the gass and water wood do that was in it. But it wood not do. He had to get gass and water to his own cost. He got a Larg Boyler 14 hors power and he had to Builde a Chimney to the Building. The Chimney and Boyler Cost him about one hundre pounds and if he Could aford it wood take one hundre pound more to finish it, Besides what he gave for his mashenery. Things are very Dull at presant and if he will Be able to meat his Calls we will be Sadsfied.

Dear Laurence, Trade is very Slack in England at presant on acount of the rumers of ware [*war*] and things are not Settled yet.[2]

Dear Laurence, I never got an answer to the Letter I sent to youkle [*your uncle*] John and that made yus [*us*] to neglect righting to you so long, waiting to get an acount from him. He Changed very much from the opinion I had of him. He is not lik me. I was Regoised [*rejoiced*] to heare from him and I thought I could corispond with him often and he was very well natured when he was at home. But he has changed very much. John and his wife is well and Doing well.

Nomore at Presant

from your Afectonate Mother Sister and Brother
untill Death

We send The Nation news pape[r]. All the news about the holy fathers Death is in it.[3]

3. *William Reynolds to Laurence Reynolds*

281 Regent Road
Salford
Dec 2/78

Dear Brother,

I received Willies Letter and I was vary glad to See you ware all well and also Willie having got on so wale at School. I falt Sorry when I read your Letter of Bernard's death. I hope God will Spare the rest of your children to grow up to be men to help and assist you and Maryann.

Dear Brother,

Trade is vary Bad in England at present. It naver was known to be so Bad before. The Cotton Iron and Building Trades are allmost at a stand-still and public opinion is vary mutch against the working man at present. Nearley all imployers Say the Men have Brought it on thamselves. Thay have Shortened the hours of work and coused wages to be advanced to that pitch that masters could get no profit, and through that the Trade has left the country and it has gone on the continant and America. For instanc the[y] can make Iron in Belgium, Send it to England, and Sell it cheeper than the[y] can in England, the Land of matel and mahinery.

Dear Brother,

My Bisness is pretty good at present, allways is about crismass. I have gust [*just*] now opened a new shop in Stratford [*Stretford*] Road, So now I have 2 shops and my works. I took the works on a Smalle leese of 3 years and I have put down large Steam Boiler with the Bed. Cost near-ley £100 pounds, than the Steam pipes and differnt other plant all cost a lot of money. In fact as fast as I could get the money I put it in plant to compete with other dyers to do the work well and quick. I have a horse and Van now and the horse mat with a great accidant about 3 weeks Since. The driver had him down and nearley Broke one knee. For a week the Vet thought he would have to be Shot But now he is get-ting better. I had to Buy another poney, So now I have two But will Sell the Big one when he is Saleable.

Dear Brother, you can see I am not without planty of work to look after for thare is allways Some Trouble turning up. And thare is a great of expensis to be mat gust [*met just*] now. At present There is between £12 and 14 pounds to be mat avery week.

Patrick is getting on vary well at the works. Maryann works as hard as aver And Mother does a lot of house work yet. She will work, will not be idle. John & wife is getting on vary well in thare Shop. Wishing you dear Brother Mary Ann and the children A Very happy Crismass and vary prosperos New Year

I remain
Yours Affactionatley
William

4. *Mary Reynolds to Laurence and Mary Ann Reynolds*

281 Regent Ro
Salford
Feb 3/79

Dear Laurence and Mary Ann,

I recived your Letter and gave me and the family great Plashure to heare you ware all well and how Willy injoyed his Little Presant from his unkle and I was very glad to heare that Previson was so chape in chicago and work getting Better.

Dear Laurence, I got a letter from your unkle John the Day I got yours and he is not so well Pleased at previson Beine so chape. He is geting a Bad Price for his hoges and cattle.

I was very glad to heare it and I hope it will continue So.

Dear Laurence, We had a very hard winter heare. Since Last november we had a hard frost and Snow and out doer woork was all Stoped and times was very Bad. Onley for the money that was Subscribed the Poore wood Be starved. Their was a lot of Soop chitchins in Manchester and Salfor[d]. In fact all England felt it.

And a great deale of the Poverty was their own fault when the[y]

Earned good waidges the Spent it in the Publick houses.

Our busness is a Bit Slack at presant on acont of the woork been slack.

Dear Laurence, We got 2 picturs from Brother John his Sons and his Doughter. He said he Did not heare from you Sence he wrote Last. He said he wood goe Down to See you.

John and his wife is well.

No more at Presant

> But Remans your
> Afectionate Mother
> Sister and Brother
> until Death

PS I hope Jonney will not forget his granmother that and pray for her.

5. *Mary Reynolds to Laurence and Mary Ann Reynolds*

> 281 Regent Road
> April 28th 79

Dear Laurence and Mary Ann,

I Recived your Letter and we ware glad to Hear that you ware all well.

Dear Laurence, I woud answer your Letter Before this But I was very ill myself and I was waiting to get Better. I am a Little Better now thanks Be to God for all his Blessings to us.

Dear Laurence, This winter was a very Severe winter and a great many old People Died hear. But the weather is Beginning to get a Little Better.

Dear Laurence, You Said in your Letter that we made a greate Mistake in the line of mens wages in England. We mad no mistake. You no [*know*] nothing about the wages the men get heare. We will Spake about our owne. Your Brother Patrick wood Be as well of[f] as William If he Kept of[f] the Beer. He had more than a few pence a week. He had from 26 s to 30 s aweek and he onley a labmaring [*labouring*] man. He worked in the Best Shop in the town, Whitworths.

We Know more about woork people. We had an Experinc of them. Your Brother William was giving a man 3.5 s aweek and in the midle of the week when he wood be in a hury to get the woork Ready he wood leave him in the midst of it and get Drunk and the next Day come in like a man that was mad and Spoile a lot of woork. One of the Best men in the trade in England.

Your Brother John Since he gave over Drinking he is a Diferent man. He has 3 hundred pounds in Bank and If he was Drinking he wood not Be worth a farthn. That is anough for us.

William is getting on prety well. He has anough to Do to Pay his Calls. One Shop is not Doing much at presant and it is a Draw Back to him.

Dear Laurence, I got a letter from the great O Toole[4] Before I got yours and I Sent him a Letter and he has not answered yet.

Let us Know all Particulars in your next Letter How you are Getting on.

No more at Presant

> But Remains
> Your Afectionate
> Mother an[d] Sister
> and Brothers
> until Death

6. *Mary Reynolds to Laurence and Mary Ann Reynolds*

> 281 Regent Rd
> Salford
> Manchester
> August 25th 79

Dear Laurence & Mary Ann,

We Recived your Kind Letter on the 15th and we ware very Happy to Hear that you ware all well as we are all well at presant, thanks Be to God for all his Blessings to us.

Dear Laurence, We ware very glad to Heare that trad was Better in America & previson chaper [*provision cheaper*].

Mary Ann and Myselfe was in Ireland for about 10 Days. The weather was very wet. We Had a Shocking Sommer this yeare. We had not One week of Drie weather all this Somer. The crops are all Damaged, the hay was all lost.

Brother Williams[5] crop was very good. If He got 3 weeks good weather hee wood Be at no loss, his land is so rockey and Drie. He is very comfortable. He has 3 Sons & 2 Dauters. One Son is in a grocers Shop in Mohill. His oldest Son is a very nice young man and the oldest Daughter went out to America 4 years agoe to her unkles her mothers brother to Kintuckey. The[y] are very well of[f] and she Sent a lot of money Home. Their name is Shannon.

Sister Sicily[6] is Doing very well. She Sent 5 of her children to America. 2 Sons ar maried there. She Lost a very fine young man 21 years old and about 14 stone. Said he was onely Sick a Short time about 12 months agoe.

We Had no Letter from Brother John Since January 25. I Do not Know what is the Mater with him. He said he wood Send his Likeness in Spring. When you goe to see him Bring all particulars. Have a good Look around and See what sort of a place he has.

Dear Mary Ann, I was very glad to Heare from you and that your baby was so good and your Health was Better. I hope God will leav him to you & I was very Much Pleased how William is getting on and how He helped you. I hope God will Bless him & Make him a good man and all the children. I will conclude By send[ing] our love to yo all.

7. *Mary Reynolds to Laurence and Mary Ann Reynolds*

281 Regent Rd
Salford
March 31st 80

Dear Laurence & Mary Ann,
    We Recived your Kind Letter and we ware glad to Hear that you ware all well as we are all well at present, Thanks Be to God for all his

Blessings to us. I am getting a great Deal Better My Selfe. I can walk about now without the Helpe of any thing and goe to Chapple the Same as Ever in the mornings. I Had a good Bill to pay the Dr But it Did not Signify when I got over it Sow Soon.

William is Doing prety well in His Busness at presant. He was Delited when you Sent the papers to Heare of the grand repshepion [*reception*] that Parnell and Dillen got in Chicagoe.[7] We have great Exitement Hear today. The Election is going of on Thursday the 1st of April. We think that the Librals will get in this time.

William Has 2 vots one in Salford & one in Manchester. He is voting for the Librals this time. He is geting disgusted with the Tories.

We got a Letter from Lizzie OToole unkle Johns Doughter the Day we got yours. She Said that the[y] ware all well and She Said She gets Letter often from you. She Said that the[y] ware making colections for the Distress in Ireland their.

Dear Laurence, We Had very good weather all this month. We had not a Drop of Rain Since the 3d of march until this morning. The weather was grand for the farmers. If it wood continue we wood Have a Early crop this yeare and it wood Be very much wanted in Ireland.

Dear Laurence & Mary Ann, I was very Sorry to Hear about Willies leg Been Hurted. He must not play with noty [*naughty*] Boys But always ceep away from them and Be a good Boy Himselfe.

John & his wife are Doing well and Keeping Stedy without the logger [*lager?*] Beer.

I have nothing more to Say at presant.

We all Joine in Sending Our Kind Love to you Mary Ann & children.

Your afectionate
Mother Sister & Brothers
until Death

8. *Mary Reynolds to Laurence and Mary Ann Reynolds*

281 Regent Rd

Oct 18 – /80

Dear Laurence & Mary Ann,

We Recived your Kind Letter & cartes.[8] We ware glad to Hear that you ware all well as we are all in at presant, thank god.

Dear Laurence, we wood not Delay so Long in Answering your Letter but we ware very Busy and William was in Ireland when we got your Letter.

William and John was in Ireland on a visit for a few Days in the Co Wicklow and the[y] ingoyed them Selves very much. It is a most Beautiful place. The Scenery is grand. No place like Dear Old Ireland.

Dear Laurence & Mary Ann, we ware Surprised when we Seen Willies cart. He lookes So Big. He is getting a fine young man for his age. I Hope He will Soon be able to Help you. We ware glad to Heare that Mary Ann ingoyed Herself so much in unkle Johns and his wife was So Kind to Her.

We got no answer from Lizzie O Toole yet. We Expect She will not forget us.

Dear Laurence, we are all in good health at presant and we have plenty of woork.

Patrick is working for William and he is Doing very well. He has taken a good deale of the work of[f] William. We opened an other shop in Harpurhey neer the queens park. It is a very nice Shop, £30/ a year and taxes. I think it will do well in time. It is not Doing very much yet But we Expect it will. It made us Busy this two months going Their & Back. Mary Ann Had not time to Rite a Letter Sooner, we have so much Buisness in hand. But we will not neglect it the next time.

John & his wife is well and ingoying good Health and Doing very well.

We had Splendid weather up to this time. It will make things chaper Both hear and in Ireland. We have great Doings in Ireland about the Land. The[y] are Shooting Some of the Big goons [*guns*]. We had a Report this morning one Shot at.[9]

I Have nothing more this time to tel you. Mary Ann is well. She has not forgot her Sister[10] in america.

No more at presant

But Remains
your afectionate Mother Sister & Brothers
until Death

9. *Mary Ann Reynolds to Mary Ann Reynolds (née Kavanagh)*

281 Regent Rd
Salford
Feb 10th 1881

Dear Mary Ann,

I Recived your Kind Letter and card from Willey which gave us great pleashure to heare that you & Laurence and the children ware all well as we are in the ingoyement of good Health at presant, thanks Be to god.

Dear Mary Ann, we had a very Severe winter the most Severest that was for 20 or 50 years. The frost was Something Dreadful while it Lasterd 3 week very Severe. It was as Bad as America. I think it was worse because we had a very heavy fogg with it. We have very heavy Rains for the Last Week. So you may think what a very unhealthy countray this is to live in.

Dear Mary Ann, we have great Debating about Ireland in parlimen[t].[11] I supose you get all the newse in chicagoe. It is Something Dreadfull how the ministers is going on. By the time you get this Letter the coercion Bill will Be pased for Ireland. The most Shamefullest Bill Ever was pased in a Sevelised [*civilised*] countray By a lot of Tory Land Lords. The[y] Have taken poor Mr Davitt[12] up Last week. He is in a convicts sell [*cell*] now. The[y] had not pations [*patience*] to wate for the Bill to Be pased Before the wood do their Dirty work. It is to be Hoped that America will Do Something now for when the Bill Be pased we Expect that a lot of the Land League will [be] put in prison. We had a great meetin Last night in the Manchester free trade hall Last night.[13] It was full to Excess and as many more out Side. It was calling on the English people to protest against the goverment in pasing the coercion Bill. Mr. Silivan[14] M.P. and Mr Dillon M.P. mad[e] gran[d] speeches The countrary [*country*] is very much Excited at presant. The goverment is trying all the[y] can to get up plots against the Irish in England to cause ill feeling Bettween Both partys. One time it will Be a feenion out Rage, an other time the[y] are going to Blow up all the Barickexs in England. We had an Explosion in Salford Barix But the[y] took all the aminicon and powder away before the Explosion took place and the[y] said it was a feenion out Rage after doing it themselves.[15] When we heard it we [k]new it was all a plot of their ow[n] making.

Dear Mary Ann, Trade was very Slack Since the knew [*new*] yeare Set in. We ware Slack But we think it was the weather Been so very cold.

John & his wife is well and Doing well. When he Seen your Letter he was proud to hiere what a big man his name Sake Jonney is. He is Sending him a presant of a prayer Book and he Hopes he will live to Be a great man and a home rooler like his unkles in Manchester.

Dear Mary Ann, William Sent a Letter to Lizzy OToole when I sent you the Letter Before cristmas. The[y] war Both posted same time and a nice cristmas cards in it and She never answered it yet. He feels very much hurt. I think She mite think it worth hir while to answer it.

Mothers health is prety good. She was not So good in the frosty weather. She is beter now.

Mother William & Patrick goyn in Sending their Love to you Laurence & the children.

M. A. Reynolds

I was Delighted with Willies gift. I will not forget it.

10. *Mary Reynolds to Laurence and Mary Ann Reynolds*

281 Regent Rd
Apr 4ᵗʰ 1881

Dear Laurence & Mary Ann,

We recived Mary Anns Letter and we ware very glad to Hear that you ware all well. We would have answered it Sooner but I was very ill myselfe. Mary Ann has been very ill for 3 weeks with a bad cold. I had rhumatic in my back. I could not goe out for 6 weeks until yesterday. I went to mass. The weather was very severe this winter. A great many people died and the weather keeps very cold yet. William and Patrick keeps well.

William got a Letter from Lizzie O'Toole the week we got Mary Anns letter and when he read it he was so disgusted with it he would not answer it. She never excused her selfe for not answering it or mintioined the presant he sent hir until the end of the Letter and made nothing of it. The Letter William sent he sent it from all the love of his heart and he expected a kind Letter comming so fare.

Mary Ann answered it for him and the[y] will open ther eys when the[y] get it. I wood like to send you a copy of it but she is not so well and it would take her to[o] long to write it. I think the[y] dont corrospond much with any one for the letters the[y] sent we have to pay for nearly all of them.

Lizzie said in hir Letter that she sent a large box of things to you for your cristmas dinner and you said you never got them. We did not like the style she termed it. Let us know in your next Letter all about it.

We dont expect to heare any more from them except thru you and I think they are not worth hearing from. When you found them out first nothing pleased me so much. I thought John would write often to me but he has not sent a Letter this 3 years.

William is sending a cross & a meddle of the Knock apration[16] and you will see it by looking thrugh the little glass in the cross, and he is sending a card of his van and horse and driver to see what you think about it. I have nothing mor to say at presant. John and wife is well and doing well. Williams work is geting a Little busyer. Write soon. No more at presant

                                                              but remans
                          your afectionate mother sister & brothers

11. *Mary Reynolds to Laurence Reynolds*

                                                              [no date]
Dear Laurence,

   Yo Said that Willie was up at his unkles in youre Last Letter. I suppose that he brought a Lot of news back. He ought to be doing well now for American Bacon is very Deare. Hear it is 10 d a pound. So he will be piling up his Dollars.

   Dear Laurence, I was thinking about you. You Should Send Willie to a trade of som discription. He is old anough now. If you Keep him any longer at Home he will be geting Idle. He ought to be bringing in Some Money to help you. You had to goe to worke very Early. William went to worke when he was 10 or 11 years at the most.

   Let us Know if you have your House and Land all pade of[f] and Send a Good Long Letter and if you are to tired Willie will rite it for you. He ought to be a good riter now. I have no more to Say this time. Rite soon.

                          Youre affectionate Mother Sister and brothers

12. *Mary Reynolds to Laurence and Mary Ann Reynolds*

                                                     281 Regent Rd
                                                     Salford
                                                     May 10th 1881
Dear Laurence and Mary ann,

   We recived your two Letters, one this Morning & one of Little Josefs Death a Day or two after we Sent the Last Letter. We ware very Sorry to heare of his Death. It would Be very hard for Mary Ann and you to part with him but gods will Be done and I hope you will Be Reconsiled about him. He is gone to heaven and I hope god wil Spare you the other three.

Dear Laurence, we are all prety well at presant. I got a good dale of Sickness this winter Myselfe. The weather was very Severe. A great many paple Dyed this winter.

Williams Busness is geting Busy and we will Expect to Be Busy for Some weekes.

Patrick is going on well and he is a great help to William and very atentive to his work. John and his wife are well an[d] Doing well. The[y] ware very Sorrey to heare of Josefs Death.

The weather is geting good and we hope we will have a good Somer.

Dear Laurence & Mary Ann, we have nothing more to say this time. We ware glad that Thomas got Better and I hope that Willie will Be a good Boy and Be able to asist his father Soone.

We all joine in Sending our Love to you all.

Your afectionate Mother Brothers & Sister

until Death

13. Mary Reynolds to Laurence Reynolds

295 Stretford Road

Manchester

Sept 1881

Dear Lawrence,

I received you[r] Letter and I was very glad to hear that you ware all well as we are all quite well at present. I would have answered your Letter Sooner but for been So Bussey. I was very glad to hear that 2 of your Sons went on a visit to uncle Johns. You Sent two of uncles Johns Letters and it is twenty years since I heard that he was getting on well and I dont Wonder at him been weld to do [being well-to-do] now I hope the children will come back in good Health and have Some very good presents beack with tham. When he sent a letter to use [us] I had 7 d to pay for it. That was not mitch friendship for his Sister. You ware vaxed with use [us] when his daughter sent use [us] a Soucey [saucy] Letter.

William was in Ireland three or four weeks ago [and] went [to his] uncles Williams. Thay ware all in good health and seem to be prospering and every thing seems to be getting on well with tham at present. I hope that John O Toole will be better to you than he was to his father as his Brother William said to my William that thare never was a more ungretefull Son crossed the water then he was to his father, as Willie Said that if his father had thrown the money in the deep he Shoud never have forgot him.

Dear Laurence, you did not menction the kind of Business your Son was at. I hope he is not in a liquor Store as anything like that it might be the ruin of him. If you could make a good Tradesman of him he would be able to get his living warever he went to.

James Curran[17] Called to See us. He is back again from America. He has Star[te]d in the provission business in Chaple Street Ancoats and he is doing well. He told us that the most foolish even in America are Irishmen keeping Thare Sons to School till thay [are] nearley young men and than thay are fit for nothing but to be corner Boys. He told us this before you even menchoned anything of you[r] Son going to work. I dont expect that anything of that Sort will ever come of any of your familey.

John is Doing well now. He has added another Shop to his business and now he has one of the best business in Manchester.

> No more at present from
> your effectionate mother

All goin in Sending our Love to you maryann and the Children.

14. *William Reynolds to Laurence Reynolds*

> 281 Regent Rd
> Salford
> Dec 4th 81

Dear Brother,

Received your letter on the 15th and we ware very grieved to read of the sad accident Mary Ann met with. I am sure it must have been a great trial for [*illegible*] for you both but I hope by the help of God by the time you receive this Letter she will be quite recovered. The reason I have not answered your Letter before this is I have had a very bad thumb, my right thumb. I got a splinter in it about 4 week since and it is very bad yet and I cannot use it [or] do any work. It is getting a little better and I have it wrapped up at the present time, and Dear Brother worse still we had Patrick bedfast for 5 weeks with rhumatic fever but he is just on the mendinghand now. It was a great loss to us to have Patrick ill so long and having a doctor comming to see him every day. My mothers health is very good considering her age and all her trouble. Mary Ann and John and his wife are all in good health.

The state of the country is about the same as before. The big bugs dont seem to know what to do. Thay are at a stand still at the present.

I suppose we will have a riot very shortley for thay put all the clever men they could lay hands on in prison.[18] That was thay last resort. We will see what they will do next.

I hope Willey will be a good boy and able to assist you very shortley. I know Mary Ann and you have had a very hard pull and a great deal of sorrow.

Inclosed is a post office order for the sum of £2.0. It will help to meet some of your expencis. I hope that you and Mary Ann and all the children will have a very Merry Cristmes and a happy New Year.

We all goin in sending our Love to you Mary Ann and the children.

Your Afectionate Brother
William

15. *Mary Reynolds to Laurence and Mary Ann Reynolds*

281 Regent Rd
Salford
Feb 6th 82

Dear Laurence & Mary Ann,

We Received your two Kind Letters which gave us great pleashure to Hear that you ware all well, particulary Mary Ann getting over all hir trouble and Having a young Doughter.[19] This time I hope god will keep her alive to Help her Mother. I was glad whin we got your Letter to See that it was a doughter, although the Mothers in America likes the Sones Because one day the[y] may get to Be the President of the great Republick of America if the[y] worke themselves up to that posison in life. It all Depends on there own Energy.

Dear Laurence, Patrick is able to goe to His worke. He was 12 weeks at Home. He is just getting Round now. Williams finger is quite well, But on christmas Eve he was coming home from the Shops after paying the girls and he tooke a cab to take him Home quick and when he was getting out his foot Sliped of[f] the Step and he Strained his foot and he could not wair his Boot for 3 weeks. We ware very thankfull, it might have Been worse. It is all Right now, thank god.

Dear Laurence, The weather is very mild. We Had no Winter this yeare. It is Like Somer weather. A great Many people are dieing this yeare. The weather would be Much more Seasonable if we had Some frost and Snow. My Health is Midling considering My age, I cannot complane. John and his wife is very well and Doing well.

Things are going on just the Same if not worse in Ireland. The[y] are filling the jails up and the people are as Determand as Ever. The[y] never ware So determand. We Expect the[y] will throw this goverment out this time. We had a great meeting in the free trade Hall. It was a grand sucess. We had Miss Parnell.[20] She Spoke well But she is getting tired out with Spaking. William and Mary Ann was on the platform. Mary Ann had the pleashure of Spaking to Miss Parnell.

Dear Laurence, We have nothing more to Say this time. I was very plased to Hear how good Willie was when his Mother was Sick. I hope he will always be a good Boy and pray for his granmother.

I Remane

youre afectionate Mother Sister & Brothers

until Death

16. *Mary Reynolds to Laurence and Mary Ann Reynolds*

> 281 Regent Rd
> Salford
> March 29th — 82

Dear Laurence & Mary Ann,

We take the opportunity of writing to you Hoping to find you and the family in good Health as the Departure of this Leaves us all in good Health, thank god for all his Blessings to us. I cannot complane of My health. It is prety good considering My age. The winter was very Mild until a week agoe and it got very cold and Stormie and wet.

William is going on very well in his Buisness. He got more new mashinary He got a new Engine. He will Be able to Do More wourke with Less Laber. It was very hard on Patrick to Do Some of the worke. It will be Much Easier now.

The trade in England is on the whole very Slack. Things are going on the Same in Ireland. Old Buck shot[21] is putting them in as fast as Ever. It all Depends on the people to keep to the no Rent Manifesto[22] until the[y] Let all the Suspects out of prisen. We would Send you Som of the Manchester papers but the[y] are all Lies. You would be Disgusted with them running Ireland down.

William Said he was glad to See that you had Such a good paper as the Citizen in chicagoe. It is a fine paper and has all the Irish newse in it. We get the Irish papers Every week and we Know how things are going on there. The Irish people heare that dose not get the papers from home, the[y] know nothing about Irelan[d] as neare as it is to England because the English papers canot be trusted.

Mary Ann Send Many thanks to Willie for his nice card and She Said that he is getting on well with his writing.

John and his wife is very well and Doing Well.

When you write Let us Know when you heard from unkle John or his family or if you got a box of things at cristmas. We would Like to Know how the[y] are going on supposin we do not write to them. Still we would Like to Know how they are going on.

Let me know how Little Mary is going on and all the Children. Write Soone and Send us all particulars.

We all joyne in Sending our Love to you all.

> Youre Afectionate Mother Sister and Brothers
>
> until Death

17. *Mary Reynolds to Laurence and Mary Ann Reynolds*

> 281 Regent Road
> Salford
> June 22nd 82

Dear Laurence & Mary Ann,

We received youre Letter and we ware vary glad to Heare that you ware all well as the Departure of this Leaves us all in good Health, Thank God for all his blessings to us.

Dear Laurence, Things are going on heare about the same. Trade is not So brisk but we Kept on pretty bussy until this Month Set in. We are Slack now and will be for a few Monthes.

All the talk in the papers is about Ireland at presant.[23] You will Have all the news in America as Soon as we get it. An other Landlord Shot, a Mr Burke.[24] He was not a very good one. The[y] keep getting poped [*popped*] down. It is breaking there Hearts.

The Grand Exabition that will be opened on the 15 of August, the goverment will try all the can to put a stop to it[25] when none of the royal family would be Let open it. We can Do vary well without royalty in Ireland. The[y] never Done anything for Ireland but punis the people and Make Emigrants of them.

There will be a Lot of people comming from America to See the Exabition. It will be a grand thing for Ireland.

There would be no use of you thinking of comming. You are so fare away and it would be very Expencive. By all accounts trade is very good in America. There are a great Many going from Ireland to it.

We had a Dreadfule Account in yester Days paper from it. A tornado in Missouri Kansas and iowa, 100 Lives Lost. We ware thinking that unkle John must have Suffered by it if we Dont heare from him. Still I will feele very unasy that any thing Should Happen to any of the family. America must be a Dreadful countrary to Live in, There are So Many great tornadoes in it.

Dear Laurence, My Health is pretty good, I canot complane. I am thinking to goe to See the old countrary this Somer if God Spars me and Mary Ann William and John are going first if all is well.

There are a great Many changes in Manchester Sinc you went away. Daniel Mahor came back from Austrlia on a visit. He is going back again. He is not Maried. James is Doing well. He has 4 children alive. Daniel Lead a very wild Life in the[y] place the call the bush.

When you get this Letter write and Let us Know [how] the[y] are all in Wisconsen and if John has got Maried yet. The[y] are doing a great buisness by all acounts. I Suppose that Mary Ann will be going up to Spend a few weeks with them Later on in the Somer. The farming buisness is Doing well in America. American cheese and bacon is up very High in this countrary [*country*].

Sence this month came in we had nothing but rain nearley Every Day. It will be very bad for the farmers if it continues. It will Make botatoes very bad and Every Kind of previson Dear.

Dear Laurence, I think I have nothing More to Say this time. John and his wife are well. As for his family the[y] are not very numers. Enclosed is a Little Sash for Little Mary. I hope she will Live to ware a many a one. I would Like to Know what you are going to put Willie to. He is getting a big boy now. I suppose he would Like the farming buisness. Right Soon and Send Me all particulars.

We all join in Sending our Kind Love to you Mary Ann and the children.

> Youre Affectionate Mother Sister and brothers
> until Death

18. *William Reynolds to Laurence Reynolds*

[October 1882?]

[*beginning missing*]

to the convention.[26] It was heald in the Leeds Town Hall. It was a vary grand assembledge. To See tham in the Streets when we adgurned at noon for Some refreshments you would think thay ware all gentlemen. The people of the Town Stood and ware supprised and could not beleve it was a meeting of Land Leaguers. There ware some vary great sweels [*swells*] from London but the most enlightened and best Speakers ware from Manchester and the Districts. Mr T P O'Connor[27] presided and he is Very Clever and everything went on as smoted [*smooth?*] as possable. The Convention was over at 5/30 and he Said it was the grandest meeting of Irishmen ever heald in England. Mr Parnell Sittled all the business in about a quarter of an hour. A good maney of the dalagates did not agree with him. I think he done the Best thing. The hole business of the League in England will be managed by about 7 Members of Parliament instead of 50 men been on the Committe as last year. I think it will go on better with a Small number having the management. Thare ware 5 or 6 Members of Parliment at the Convention. Mr Sexton[28] is a Very Clever man. He is one of the Cleverest men I have ever herd Speak and to look at him you would be supprised at the ability he is possesed of.

Dear Brother, The men at the Branch[29] here Tryed Very hard to get me to run for counsellor for ArdSal [*Ordsall*] ward, and some of the principle man in Manchester, Some Docters committed with the League, but I would not undertake it. I promised to undertake it in 2 or 3 years from now. I mite be able to give Some of my time to it. For a man to accept a post of that Sort he wants to be a man of ability and a good deal of expearance. Thay said I was the only Irishman in Salford thay would like to Bring forward.

Dear Brother, At present I have as mutch to do as is vary good for my health and constitution. I have nothing else I can tell you about at present except the change thare has come over Manchster Since you left. I dont know what has become of your old companions. James Curran came from America. He called to See Patrick and I at the works and we had a long chat. He was Supprised how I got on. He could not make out how it was done. He was in grand health. He lost Some of his fingers wile in the States working a curculer Saw. He only came over on a visit but he told us after a time he will Come and Settle in Manchester.

Dear Brother, I was very glad to See by your Letter that you are looking after the aducation of your Children. You could not do anything Better for without aducation at the present Day people are simply nothing in the World. Inclosed is a Cabinet[30] of me mothers and a small card of Patricks. Thay ware not ready the last letter I had sent. Nomore at present. All goin in Sending thare love, Mother Mary Ann and Patrick to you Mary Ann and the Children.

Your effectionate Brother
William

19. *Mary Reynolds to Laurence and Mary Ann Reynolds*

[December 1883?]

[letter torn across the top]

Dear Laurence & Mary Ann,

I Recived your Kind Letter and we ware very glad to Heare that you war all well as we are all well at presant, thank Be to God for all his Blessings to us. You will think me very unkind for not writing to you Before this But we ware very Busy. William was opening an other new Shop neare the queens park about 5 miles from where we Live and all their time was Spent going theire and Back. It is a very nice Shop and we

[one line torn off]

We had a letter from Lizze OToole the Same time I got youres and we had no time to answer it yet But I will send hir one now. She said in her letter that James *[the word 'Willie' is crossed out]* was up and he was a fine Smart Boy of his age. She did not call him William. She called him James and we ware wondering whou it was. If you did not till us in your Letter about Willie going up we woul[d] not Know who it was.

William was Disapointed. he thought his name was William.

[one line torn off]

I am afraid the harvest will Be Lost in England & Ireland agane this yeare. The rain is Something Dreadful and thunder Storms. We had a great thunder Storm in Manchester and loss of Life.[31] Two shops ware Blooen Down. All over England their was great Damage done.

A pilgrimage left Manchester yester Day for Ireland county Mayo to Our Lady of Knock. It was a grand site to see them, about 600. Some wair lame, some Blind. I hope they will come back

[two lines torn off]

Dear *[torn]* Losses in our Busness. We lost 4 horses in about two years. William got a new van. It is the nicest van in manchester. He gave 40 pond for it. Our Busness is profitable with all the losses, Sow we must not complain. I have nothing More to Say this time. In your next Letter send all particulars about unkil John and Let us Know has he many people working for him. I think he is not in a very large way. Now more at present

But Remains
your afectionate Mother Brother & Sister
until Death

20. *Mary Reynolds to Laurence and Mary Ann Reynolds*

> 295 Stretford Road
> Manchester
> Feb 4th— 84

Dear Laurence and Mary Ann,

I hope you will Excuse us for not answering youre letter before this. We ware So busy Since we came to Stretford Road we had hardley time to do halfe of what we had to do. The Shop is So Large it wants a Lot of Looking after. William was busy getting circulars ready. He got 30 thousant printed for all the Shops. The[y] cost a Lot of Money but we Expect the[y] will bring Some work in. Trade is not So good as it has been. The Scotch dyers are doing all the[y] can to get the trade of Manchester, putting their Sines up Every place the[y] can get a chance. So it will take us all Our time to wach them. Our shop is the nicest dyers shop in Manchester.

Dear Laurence, we are all in pretty good health. The weather has been Very Mild. We had no frost or Snow this winter but we had two great Storms don great damage in Ireland and England. We thought the House would be blowen down on[e] night, the Storm was So great.

John and Bridget is in good Health and doing well. We had James Curran back from America again.

I will Send you one of the circulars to See what you think about it.

Dear Laurence, it was on this day of the Month that you Left us 4th of Feb.

It seems a Long Time.

I have nothing More to Say this time. Hoping this will find you and Mary Ann and the children in good health, we all Send our love to you Mary Ann & the childern.

> Youre affectioonate Mother
> Sister and Brothers

Write Soon

21. *Mary Ann Reynolds to Laurence Reynolds*

295 Stretford Road

Manchester

Sept 8/ 86

Dear Brother & Sister and children,

We Received youre Letter Last week and it gave us very great pleashure to hear you ware all well and doing So well. We Received all the Letters you Sent and papers. You had great meetings in chicago.[32] I hope the[y] will do Som good for poor Old Ireland for it is in a very poor State at presant, never was much worse.

Dear Brother, You ware Surprised that we did not answer your Letters. We thought it better not. The other last letters gave Mary Ann So Much trouble. The[y] ware all wrote at Mothers dictation and the[y] ware not Sent to cause any trouble. Mother thought She was giving a good advice. We always have taken her advice and we hav not gon very rong.

Dear brother, I will tell you about Mother. She has been very ill for the Last 16 monthes. She has not beent to Mass onley about 3 times. Severel times we thought She would die, She was so bad. She keeps very poorley yet. She will never get strong again. I think the doctor Says it is the weasting of her Sistom [*wasting of her system*].

William & Patrick ar going on very well. William is Enlarging his buisness very Much. He has taken a lot of ground that goins his works and Let it into it, So it is the Largest about Manchester. He Spent a lot of Money to fit it up. Trade has been very Slack hear for a very long time. Manchester was nearley all to let or to be Sold, trade was so bad, thousants out of employment. We could not complane, we Kept prety busy all along.

John is doing very well. I think I told you he bought a little property. He was very looky [*lucky*]. He had all his houses taken but he is thinking to sell his buisness in about an other 12 monthes and the[y] will have a rest for a while. He may go to Ireland, Somplace neare the Sayside. I was in Ireland for my holidays about a month agoe. I went to the Same place, bray, but John went to corrick. You will be Surprised when I tell you of unkle Williams death Last Spring. He was no time Sick. The winter was so Severe he god cold and could not get over it. He had a grand funeral. John stoped for about 10 days with them. The[y] ar very lonley. All the old stock is dieing out. When you write to unkle John tell him about unkles death.

Dear Brother, When you send the next Letter tell us about unkle and his family or has John got married. We like to know how the[y] all are. We have dreadful newse from America about the earthquake in Charless town.[33] It was awful to read it. It is much safer to be living in England. We have a lot of rain in this country. We had not 5 weeks of hot weather this sason, all rain and cold. We thought their would be no harvest but we had about 10 hot days and it was very hot while it lasted. We thought we wair going to have the American weather. We wair nearley rosted but it did not last long. It is much colder now.

Dear Brother, I think I have nothing more to tell you. Wishing you and Mary Ann every prosperity in your new shop. And I am shure I have no need to speak about James William. He is very enterprising for his age. He will say their is nothing like a little bit of buisness after all. I hope Mary Ann will not forget Mother in he[r] prayrs. We all Send our love to you Mary Ann and the children.

Youre affectionate Sister
Mary Ann
and Mother and Brothers

22. *Mary Ann Reynolds to Mary Ann Reynolds (née Kavanagh)*

Manchester
Feb 15th 1888

Dr Sister,

I hope you will forgive me for not answering your letter before this. I was very ill this two monthes. I had to have medical advice and the doctor Said I was nearley leting myselfe go to[o] long. I am much better now, thank god. Mother keeps about the Same. She got over the winter wonderfull. I think She will be able to go out this Sommer if god Spears her to us. William & Patrick is very well and John and bridget is very well and doing well.

Dear Sister, we ware glad to heare that you and Laurence and the family ware in good health and that James is doing So well.

Trade is very bad in England at presant. Onley for the Ship canal[34] that started in Manchester, thing[s] would be very bad. We will have all the Shipping coming into Manchester instead of Liverpool and it is Sure to Stir trade up. We have a lot of Money invested in building Societys & their would be no posibility in getting it if the Ship canal did not start. The company that has the Management of it will buy a lot of property.

The Exabition[35] was a Great Success. It brought a lot of people to Manchester while it lasted. We have a lot of your fokes over heare. I think you will know them. The great wild west Show buffalo bills or the Honerable W. Cody.[36] He is the talk of Manchester. He is a very fine looking man and a catherlick. He was born near to wher unkle John OTooles place is. He has a lot of indians with him. The[y] dont like Manchester, it is so damp and foggie, it is not like west of America. We have don Some work for them and Miss Cody. She is a nice lady.

Dear Sister, things are very bad in Ireland.[37] The[y] keep going from bad to worse. The goverment is a disgrace to aney civilized country the way they are going on but it cant go on Much longer.

I havenot herd from home this 6 monthes. I thought to write befor Chrismas but I was not able. I will have to comence and send a letter to all of them.

Dear Sister, I think I have not got much more to tell you. Write and let us know how you are going on in your Shop and send a good letter (Laurence wont Send Much if he writes it) and Send a lot of news.

Mother sends her Love to you all and hopes you will pray for her. William and Patrick Joyns with me in Sending our Love to you all.

Your affectionate Sister

Mary Ann

23. *Mary Ann Reynolds to Mary Ann Reynolds (née Kavanagh)*

[November 1888?]

Dear Sister,

You would have a stormey time during the election of the Presi-
dant.[38] We had the news heare next morning after he got in. I wonder if he will do anything for the Irish or Ireland now that he has got
in.

The English wair awfully hurt about the English ambasesater been
sent home.[39] Onley they have got their hands full of the Irish question,
Their might be a bit of a fite but they have anough to do now what with
all the womon that are getting mutilated in London.[40] It is something
dreadfull.

Dear Sister, I have Sent a parcle this morning. It is a little presant to
Mary. I hope you will get it all wright. I have paid the carrage through
to Chicago. I would have sent her something sooner but the carrage is
enormus. Please let me know when you get it if it is all write. You will
haave it as soon as this letter. I hope she is a good girle. I forgot her age.
I thought that she would be about 6 or 7 years. I hope God will spare
her to you. My mother would be very lonley if she had not me. Men
are all wright in there own place but their is no one Like a daughter
when they get old. I hope that Mary wont forget to pray for her gran
mother every day for her gran mother never lets one day pass without
Saying the Rosary for Laurence & Mary Ann & her family. She is from
morning till night saying her bades. Walking or Sitting She has the bades
in her hands.

Dear Sister, I have nothing more to tell you this time. Mother
William & Patrick goines with Me in Sending our Love to you Laurence
and all the children.

Youre affectionate Sister
Mary Ann

24. *William Reynolds to Michael O'Toole*[41]

295 Stretford Road
Manchester
Jan 21/89

Dear Uncle,

I received your very kind & welcome Letter in Due time. Mother and all of us ware very glad to hear from you, cousin Mary & Husband and familey and that thay ware in good health. I beg to thank you for your nice Letter and all your good wishes and am sorry I have not replyed to it Sooner. I have been taking up in the business Since I seen you.

Mother has being getting pretty good health. She was able to go to Mass good meney Sundays before Crismess but not able to go Since. Her health vareys. Mary Ann keeps well. John keeps Strong and is going on Very Niceley in his business. Patrick & myself are quite well. We receive Letters from Laurence from time to time. He has got a familey growing up, 2 Sons working. He has got on better in Chicago laitley than he has Since he went to America.

I am going on very well in my business. It is allways rather quite [quiet] in the beginning of the year. People here Seem to think this will be a good year for Trade. I hope So and I hope Ireland will be more prosperious this year. The people in Ireland are getting punished dredfull by the Tory government and Bad Landlords but it is a long lane has no turn. The time will come for the people in Ireland I hope Very Shortley.

Since I was in Ireland I have invested my money in Some property in Hulme, a very nice block of nine houses & 2 shops. When I get all straight I will have an Income clear of expence of £100 per year besides my business. I have given £1360 for it.

Dear Uncle, I hope you Mary & Husband and all are injoying good health. Write Soon when you receive this Letter. Mother and all goin in Sending Love and best wishes. Remember me to Mr & Miss McGershin.[42]

I remain
your effectionate nephue
William Reynolds

25. *William Reynolds to Laurence Reynolds*

[*written on black-bordered stationery*]

295 Stretford Road
Manchester
Jan 2/90

Dear Brother,

I am Sorry to inform you of our Patricks Death. He died on Dec 15th after a fortnights Illness, Decese of the Heart. He died Vary Suddenly. We thought he would pull through to the last but he died in an instant. It has been a great blow to us all. Maryann was So prostrate with grief She took ill on Dec 26th with Inflammation of the Bowels and had a Narrow escape. She is gust comming round now but Still Bedfast and will be for Sometime but I think the worst is over. Mother is keeping vary well considering. She has kept up the best. I had a hard gob to keep right myself. It has been a Great blow to me to loose Patrick after all the years that him an[d] I have been togather and avery thing prospering round us. He was well attended by Priest and doctor and we done all on our power for him. John and his wife are well. John was vary Sorry and grived for the loss of Patrick to die in his prime. Thare is nothing more I can tell you this time. It has been a down a downcast Chismass for us but we are Vary Glad Maryann is pulling through. With kindest regards to Maryann and all your familey.

I remain
your Effectionate Brother
William Reynolds

26. *William Reynolds to Laurence Reynolds*

295 Stretford Road
Manchester
Sept 16th 1890

Dear Brother,

I received your Letter in due time and mother and all ware glad to hear that you and Mary Ann and all the family ware in good health and also glad to hear your Sons ware getting on So well. Mother and all of us are quite well at present. Mother is getting vary nice health. She is now in her 81ᵗʰ year. We ware glad to See you got acquainted with Sutch respectable name Sakes, Father Reynolds[43] coming to live in the same parish. I believe I knew his Brother vary well by Sight. He was a good looking young man. I hope he will get on well in Chicago in the business he was about to commence in. Kindly remember me and all the family to Father Reynolds and all our name Sakes. Thay will be all Sorry to hear of Uncle Micheals Death. When Patrick died he Sent a Letter expressing great Sorrow and Sympathy with us in loosing Patrick. He died in about two months after Patrick He was a fine old man and I hope his Soul is happy.

Dear Brother, I would have answered your Letter before but Mary Ann went to Ireland for a month for the good of her health and She returned vary mutch improved. She went to Bray Co Wicklow. It is a vary nice Sea Side place, it is called the Brighton of Ireland. Soon after She arrived home I went for my holiday. I had 3 weeks in Ireland. I stayed at Bray but I went to Kallarney to See the Lakes for a few Days. I liked Kallarney vary mutch. The Lakes are beautifull. The travvalling in Ireland is not so plesent. The trains go rather Slow and thare is vary little convenance for travvellers. I am sure the Americans comming to Kallarney will find a change. I was speaking to one myself. The Climate is so mutch different to America. This year has been vary wat up to this month September. The wheather is now beautifull. The air is is vary pure in Ireland and the Scenery beautifull.

The Country is at a Stand Still. All the governments in the past have done all thay possiable Could to stop the Country from been devaloped and done all in thair power to ruin the Country, but once Ireland gets Home Rule the Country will advance rapidley in Trade and everything. The Country Seems as if it was waiting as it ware to be allowed to advance. Thare is everything in the Country to be happy and prosperous if the people ware only allowed to develop it thamselves.

I am getting on vary well in my business. I have worked hard and Steady and So has Maryann but we have to thank God for how he has prospered us. John & Bridget are getting on well and in good health.

We had a Cousin from Ireland who called to See us, Marian OToole. But She is now married and her married name is McManus. She is the Matron at the Workhouse in Carrick on Shannon. Her Husband is the School Master at the same place. She has one Sister in Manchester married to a young man named Masterson. He is in the Egg & Butter line. His Father is well of[f] at home at Annaduff. He buys the Eggs and Sends tham over to his Son to Sell in Manchester. Thay are doing Vary well. We had a great Day last Sunday week. Thay Stayed all the Day with us. I had two horses & Traps out in the afternoon and we had a plesent Day. And during the week I showed tham my property and went through the works. Thay ware vary pleased with all and thay Ware Supprised to See So Mutch Machinery.

I will write you another Letter as Soon as I get a little time and Send you more perticulers. All goin in Sending thair love and best wishes to you Maryann and all the Children.

I remain
your Effectionate Brother
William

27. *William Reynolds to Laurence Reynolds*

295 Stretford Road
Manchester
Dec 8th 1890

Dear Brother,

I would have written you a Letter before but I have had so mutch to attend to I have not been able. I hope you and Maryann and all the family are injoying good health. I hope your Sons are getting good health and doing well at thair business. Chicago is a fine City. We are all getting pretty good health at present. My mother is getting as good health as can be expected. John & Bridget are quite well and doing well in thair Business. I think the Exhibition at Chicago will be a great Success.[44] Chicago seems to be a city advancing Vary rapidly. You Should

Commence Something on your acount now. It would be better than working for an imployer.

I am getting on vary well. I have plenty of work & very little play but Still I am my own master. I have about 30 persons imployed. In fact the Business is getting as mutch as Maryann & I can manage. But when people are making a little money it is some incouragement.

I received a Letter from Cousin Lizzie last June but I am Sorry I have not been able to Send an answer yet. She Sent Marthas phopto [sic]. She is a Hansome Girl. If She came to Stay with you kindley remember all to har. & Should you write to uncle John Say All in Manchester beg to be remembered to all the family.

We are having a vary exciting time at present through the dredfull Mess Mr Parnall has got into. Everything was in favour of Ireland till the O'Shea divorce case[45] came on and the Irish people ware vary united and preparing for a General Election but now a great deal of the preparation seems to be cast to the winds and it will take a long time to get tham So united again. Parnall is to be blamed for all. If he had been upright and having a proper Love for Ireland he would have retired at once. If only for a time till the devorse case was forgotten. But now I am Sorry to Say all is over with Parnall. He will never be Leader of the Irish people again. He was getting credit for what other men ware doing. John Dillon & William O'Brine[46] doing all thay possiable could for the poor tennants in Ireland, Keeping tham united and fighting the exterminating Landlords. You will See allmost as Soon as we over here how he has divided the Irish members into two Camps & I suppose the Irish people the Same. Old Gladstone[47] has been the hope of the Irish people in these Countrys. He has worked hard for Ireland to get the English people to consent to Home Rule. It is vary hard to get anything of[f] the English. Of course Old Billey in one Sence had no right to interfere in Sending his Letter. But the Liberals having worked So hard and the Irish people having worked So hard, Thare was every prospect of Home Rule from the Liberals when thay got into power. I hope all will turn out for the best Thare is one thing Sertain that Parnall was not fit to be the Leader of the Irish people after the devorse case.

I have Seen by the papers you have had great meetings in Chicago & the dalagates got a grand reception.[48] Irish people in America have Liberty. That is more than we can Say in this Country.

I must Conclude this Letter. Write Soon and Send all perticulars of how you Maryann and all the family are. All goin in wishing you a happy Crissmas and a prosperous New Year.

> I remain
> your Effectionate Brother
> William

P.S. I send you a copy of our Mothers Pedigree. The History of the Clan OToole has been writteen by the Rev P L OToole, O.C.C. of Dublin.[49] I am one of the Subscribers & my name is printed in the first addition [*edition*]. I was Speaking to him in Dublin during the Summer when over. I have got my addition. It is a splendid Book. I know you will be plesed with the copy of [it].

[*In an agitated draft of this letter to his brother, William wrote the following passages in the section about Parnell, which he subsequently deleted.*]

See how he has divided the Irish Members and people in Ireland and all over. If he had retired at once the Irish members would not have attacked [?] him very mutch and they would still have the sympathy of the world. The Bishops have given thare dissicion & deserved all. I dont See he can do anything now. He has not been looking after anything for Ireland, the Parlimantary business, for Some years. When the whole thing should have been fought to the vary end . . .

The Irish people every ware are upset. Some are for Parnell & Some are for Dillon & Obrine. The Bishops in Ireland have condemed him. He has sartenely been a Vary Clevour Leader, one of the Greatest Leaders ever Ireland had, but for some years he has not assisted his own party as well as he Should have done.

28. *William Reynolds to Elizabeth O'Toole*

295 Stretford Road
Manchester
Jan 5th 1891

Dear Cousin Lizzie,

[*William recapitulates family news contained in the foregoing letter.* Circa 275 words] We have had a great deal of excitement here over the Parnell business. It caused a great maney things to be at a Stand Still. It has been a vary bad thing for Ireland. It is like as if thare is allways Something to happan to throw Ireland back. Parnell is not fit to be the Leader again. I think myself he never will be the Leader of the Irish people again. It has been all the talk for Some time and is Still but we are getting completely tired of it and the Sooner it is Settled the better.

We got the news of the Battle with the Indians. Thay are a wild desperate race.[50] I hope thay are a long distence from your Home. The Americans Troops will quiten tham pretty quickly but not without Some li[v]es lost. I hope all my cousins are safe from tham in Texas. My mother would like to [obtain] uncles & aunts likeness. I will try and Send you more information in my next letter.

William Reynolds

All join me in wishing you all a Vary Happy & prosperous New Year.

I remain
your Effectionate Cousin

29. *William Reynolds to Mary Reynolds (Mohill)*[51]

295 Stretford Road
Manchester
Oct 26th 91

Dear Cousin Mary,

I received your Letter and We Ware all glad to hear from you and that you are getting on So well, considering the Summer was So bad for

Farming. My mother has not been so well in health but taking her great
age in to acount she keeps up wonderfull. Maryann had a vary bad illness this year. She was bedfast for a month. She got round pretty well
and went over to Bray for a month and She is now mutch better and
Stronger for the rest and the Sea air. She Caught Cold and got an attack
of inflamation of the Bowels again. John & his wife are quite well and
doing Well in thair business. I keep up vary well myself. I have not
mutch to complain of as regards health. I have as mutch as I can manage in the business. I am getting on vary well. It keeps increasing and it
requires a great deal of attention. I was in Bray for a fortnight. I stayed
at Bray Head Hotel. It is a fine place and a grand place for peoples
health.

You Speak in your Letter about your Daughter. She would like to go
to business and like to get a Situation. Let me know in your next Letter her age if She is old enough to leve Home. We have 3 young Ladies
at Stretford Road shop ware we live and this is our principle Shop. This
would be the best place for her. If She would turn out suitable and live
with us and be Smart, Maryann no doubt would make a business
woman of her. We have a great meney customers at this shop and we
do the business in the highest style, vary nessesary to carry the business
on as thare are a great meney Dyers in Manchester.

I received a Letter a few days ago from Laurences Son in Chicago.
He is getting a vary smart young man. Thay are getting on well and all
the talk at present is the wourlds Show to be hald thare in 1893.
Remember John & myself to Mr McGushin. I am vary glad [he] is Still
keeping in good health. All his family are good hearted. A great meney
of the Farmers Dye vary young Supprising and living in shutch a bea-
tuy[ful] country.

I remain
your Effectionate Cousin
William Reynolds

30. *Mary Ann Reynolds to Mary Ann Reynolds (née Kavanagh)*

295 Stretford Road
Manchester
Dec 18th 91

Dear Mary Ann:

It is a Long time since I have writton to you but I hop you will Excuse Me on acount of my illness. I am Much better now, thank God. I hope that you and Laurence and all the family are in good health. Mother William and Myselfe are very well. Mother is wounderfull for her age. She goes about the house and Keeps up Very well. She has not been out for about 2 monthes. The weather is So bad that it would not be fit for her to Step out. I hope that She will be able to go out again in the Sommer if God will Spare her to us.

Dear Mary ann, Youre family all groing up now they will be a great help to you. James is a fine young Man. We liked his Cabinet Very Much. John is looking out for one. John and his wife is doing very well and they are in good health. I think they will be giving up their buisness in the Spring. We are very busy at presant. We have a lot to do because the buisness is increasing every day & it leaves a lot of work for William and myselfe to do. It is so very hard to get men to work honest and be trustworthy.

Dear Mary Ann, Mary will be getting a fine guirle now. She must send me her likeness as I would like to see it and Mother would like very much to see it before She dies. She always likes to hear from you all and I hop you will remember her in youre prayrs. It was Patricks aniversary of his death last Sunday. May the Lord have mercy on his Soule. We had 6 Masses offered up for the repose of his Soule. I hope that he is in heaven.

The weather in England & this winter is all rain ans Strom [*and storm*]. We had a Great Hurrican about a week ago, it was Something dreadful.

[*remainder missing*]

31. *Mary Ann Reynolds to Mary Ann Reynolds (née Kavanagh)*

Dudley Place
Old Trafford
Manchester
July 19, 1892

Dear Sister,

I havnot Kept to my Promis I am Sory to Say but it is better Late than than never. I hop that you and Laurence and the family are all well. We are all well, thank God. Mother is doing very well. You will See by My Letter that we Removed to a privet house in Old Trafford. Laurence will Remember it. It is a very nice house with a Larg Garden at the back and a Small one at the frunt. We can go out of the dining room into the Garden. It will be very plesant for Mother. It is a Larg house. Their are 5 beadrooms bath &c upstairs and drawing room and dining Room Larg Kitchin and 2 other Rooms with 4 larg Sillers. It was £50 a yeare with taxes but we got it a Little Less. So you See we Keep moving on. We had the parish priest to come yesterday to bless it and he was delighted with it. It cost William a lot of Money to have it furnished with Suitable furniture. He always told Mother that he would have her in a nice house with a Garden before She died.

We done nothing but Removing Since Last April. We Removed from 295 Stretford Rd to a Shop next the works and we find it more conveniant every way. Now that we have gon to Live privet it cost a lot of money and time to fit it out. It did not interfare with the Buisness. We have been very busy all the yeare, as much as we can do. The new Shop is greatley admired, no dyers Shop in Manchester to come up to it. Their are always a crowd outside Looking at it. It is the best Side for buisness. Our trad has incrased Since we opned it.

Dear Sister, We have a great dale of Rain in this countrary. We have Scearcley aney hot weather, Raining Every day. The farmers will be at a Great Loss if we have not a chang for the better Soon.

We have great Excitement in england at this presant time with the Generale Election. Gladstone has won. I hop he will let Ireland have homrool at once and Settle all the strife. It is nearley time to do Somthing.

Dear Sister, John and his wife are very well. My health is much better this yeare. I think now as we have gon to the new house we will all get better health. The eare [*air*] is purer and not so much Smoak. And I wont ask to go for aneymore holidays. Mother is to old to be Left now.

You will have a grand time next year with the Exabition. Their will be a lot of people from hear going to See the Wourlds Show. William is talking about going but I think that he wilnot go. It is a long way from home and Mother would not like to Let him go.

Dear Sister, Send a Letter Soon, do not take example from me. I would have writon but we wair So busey. Mary will be a fine Girl now. I would like to see her pickture in your next Letter. I have nothing More to tell you this time. Mother & William joins with me in Sending our Love and best wishes to you all.

Youre Sister Mary Ann

32. *Mary Ann Reynolds to Mary Ann Reynolds* (*née Kavanagh*)

1 Dudley Place
Old Trafford
Manchester
Ap 6/93

Dear Sister and Brother and Family,

You will think it very unkind of me not answering your Letter Sooner but when I tell you all the trouble we had sence the 20th of July you will be Surprised to hear it all. After I wrote you in a week or two after one of our places was burned out, not a bit of it Left. Where we don all the dry cleaning. The Shock was So Great that we thought we would not get over it. William was very much troubled about it but thank god we are over the worst now. The loss was about £1500 pounds and we wair very Busy at the time. It was onely insured for the one third of the Loss. The clames for goods was about £250 and we Lost all the mashinary. One machine cost £100 to fit it up. So we have go[ne] through a Lot Sence Last July but thank god we havenot done So bad after all. Our coustemers wair very good, all the time Sent all their work. All the dyeing part was Saved, So we Kept our work on all the time. We had to Send the dry cleaning to an other dyer for Som weeks. The goods are cleaned with Spirits and the[y] have to be very carfull Because when it coms to a Serton heat it will with the Least friction tak fire.

The Landlord of the place would not Rebuild it for us, So William has been thinking about getting a new works for Somtime as it was not a Suitable place for dyein buisness. The countrary [*country*] is much better. William got a Place that was to be Sold and I think it will all turn out for the better. He Bought it off alltogather. Their is a Lot of Land with it. He bought it Soon after the fire, he gave £700 for it. Their was two or 3 buildings on it that he had Repaired along with building a larg new building. It will be one of the Largest in England. It has cost a lot of money. When finished it will take over £2000 pound befor it is complated. We Started som machines in it last week drycleaning. The men wair Employed at the new building about 6 months.

Last June a Son of cousin Mary Reynolds came over and William Started him as bookkeeper.[52] He is a very Stedy young man. He is about 27 years. He was 7 or 8 years with atorney Obrine[53] but he could get no money from him. He has been writon to William asking him to find him Som Employment hear. When he came over William Started him at once. We find him very usefull. We have So much corisponding, our trade is increasin very much.

Dear Sister, if you ware living near us your Sons would be a great help to the buisness as it is very heavy on William and myselfe.

Dear Sister, Mother is prety well considering. My health has been bad this winter. I was 4 weeks confind to my Room. My breathing is very short and weak action of my heart. William is prety well. I thought he would break down, the Shock was So much for him. We are all improving, thank God. John and his wife is very well.

William was thinking about going to chicago, onley we hapned with this loss. Nothing would please him better than to see the Worlds Shoe

[*World's Show*]. It will be a grand thing to See it. It is all the talk over heare, that and home Rule for Ireland.

Dear Sister, I hop by the time you get this letter that you and family will be in the injoyment of good health. I got Thomases likeness. He is a fine young man. We ware delighted with it. We would lik to See Marys next.

Dear Sister, I have nothing more to tell you in this Letter. I forgot to tell you William had two Letter from Unkle['s] two daughters telling us about their weddings but William was in So much trouble he could-not answer them. Now I finish

with Kindest wishes from
Mother William and myselfe
Mary Ann

33. *William Reynolds to Laurence Reynolds*

1 Dudley Place
Old Trafford
Manchester
Oct 19/ 1893

Dear Brother,

I take this opportunity of writing this Letter to you hopeing your-self Maryann and all the family are enjoying good health. My mother Maryann John & his wife and myself are quite well. My mother is keep-ing up wonderfull for a woman of her age and everybody is supprised she keeps So well. Wheather it is the number of prayers she says, as she is praying continually, or the great care taken of her I dont exactley know. I think one helps as well as the other to keep her living.

Maryann or myself would have written to you before. Only we have had So mutch to contend with Since our place caught fire. The amount of work we had to do was Something enormous. For myself I can Say I passed through the most trying time of my life and Just Managed to pull through with the narrowest escape of loosing our business. There was a loss alltogather with goods in trust for Dyeing & Cleaning to the extent of £1300. I received from insurence £580 but had to Settle all claims of goods out of this amount. What remained was not vary mutch.

The Landlord of place burnt out was not insured and would not rebuild allthough having plenty of money. Our business was at a Standstill and our goods had to be sent out to be cleaned elswhare. And I had to pay rentel for 12 months for old ruin. Thare was nothing for me to do but look about and find a works. I came across the old mill at Longsight and purchased it. Thare was nearly 13 hundred yards of vacant land. But the mill was vary mutch out of repair. The house on the front of Stockport Road was used as a Babtist Mission. I paid £600 for the place as it stood and it cost £300 more to repair and get into working order. The new Buildings cost about £800. I was my own contractor. It was a hard gob for me and I never want another like it. I was nearly laid up and trying to to look after our Dyeing business as well. Only I done my own contracting it would have cost me half as mutch more With the Buildings and machinery I have Sunk about £3000. I managed to hold my house property but had to borrow £1200 The Steam Boiler in old works was was too Small and had to buy a larger Boiler. The Boiler in new works 24 Feet long 6 Feet 6 dia., 8 Lubes, double flued steel ends, one of the best made, cost over £200. And the works had to be fit up with gas steam and water. And Shafting and machinery anacted in different departments. The buildings cover about 1500 yards – and is now one of the best works in England. The back of works overlook the Great Western Railway to London. It was a heavy trial to pass through. At the present time the Coal Strike has allmost all business at a Stand Still. I have been loosing about £5 per week through advanc in price of coal. When I purchased the mill there were two Tennents, The mission people and one who had part of old Mill. The mission people had 18 months of thair Lease to run and as I wanted tham out in about 3 months thare was a difficulty here to be overcome. I corrosponded with tham as I thought it was betterr than personall interviews and told tham how I was Situated – been [*being*] burnt out. I mat tham on good terms and got tham out in about 3 months. Thay removed a little lower down and built an Iron chaple on Some Vacant Land. Thay did not find out I was a Catholic till the works was finished. I heard afterwards when thay found out that I was a Catholic thay were vary annoyed.

Hughie was with me from the time of the fire. Been [*Being*] a good writer and 9 years with Attorney OBrien, his legel knowledge helped me from time to time. I am now the owener of the Longsight Mill, The only Mill in the Village. Father Daly[54] called and went through the works. When he heard all he said you are the only Irishman in Longsight and prayed that God would Bless the place and myself.

We received a Letter from Maryann and also one from James William with photo of his Brother Short time Since.

Dear Brother, John & wife have retired short time since from business and are now living at Stretford near Manchester in a vary nice House. Thay have managed to Secure an income Suffucent to Support tham. Thay have two lots of property and receive about £4 per week from tham. The last lot he bought through me. When I got the mill working thay thought I was a Millionare and I had Sevarel lots of property offered to me. The lot John bought ware a bargain and I saved him about £70 in the property. Thare are 13 houses, 4 on the front of Stockport Road in a line with mine, and 9 houses behind. He has an income from this lot of about £2–14–0 per week and perchused tham for the Sum of £850. This lot were bargein. They ware very heaviley morgaged. The owener wanted money. John bought tham at the right time. The Mill is called Spring Bank Mill and Johns houses are next to the mill and named Spring Bank View. John and I are still close togather. Hughie bought the goodwill of Johns business in Travis Street and Sent to Ireland for his Sister and Brother. Thay have been over about one month and are gatting on as well as can be expected up to the present. I am Sorry to Say Hughies Father Died Since he Hughie came to Manchester. He has been in my imploy as bookeeper Since he came over about 15 months.

Dear Brother, The Worlds Fare at [Chicago] I Suppose is nearly over. I am Sorry I had not the chance of paying a visit to see it and to see you and your family and all our friends. Nothing would have been more plesent If I could have managed it. I hope with the help of God I will be able to visit Chicago yet to see you and your wife and all the family and all our friends. Chicago is a great City and America is a great Country. Thare is more liberity in America than in England and I think the people are not So heavily taxed. It is the home of our country people. The English people are not in Sympithy with us and do not nor never did like us. Our country people are only receiving the crums wile thay eat the loaf. We ware willing to make the best use we possiable could of the Home rule bill, if the upper Supterfuge had not trown the bill out.[55]

In Maryanns letter to us She mentioned about James William comming to Manchester. Thare are a good meney things to be considered. If he has a good prospect in Chicago it would be rong to come away as I think he would be mutch happier in Chicago with his own Brothers. Maryann and I have talked it over meney a time if we could get a friend to assist us in the business as it has been vary heavy for Maryann and myself to manage from time to time. Let us know your opinion in your next Letter. If Manchester did not Suit him after about 12 months time he could return to Chicago. I am sure you will be wearied reading this Letter. I thought I would make up for lost time. All send the[ir] love and best wishes to you Maryann and all the family.

> I remain
> your Effectionate Brother
> William Reynolds

34. *William Reynolds to Laurence and Mary Ann Reynolds*

> 1 Dudley Place
> Old Trafford
> Manchester
> Dec 27/93

Dear Laurence and Maryann,

I sent you a Letter about 6 weeks ago and I have not received an answar. I expacted one. We have considered about James William comming to Manchester. And we would be all pleased If he Should come as Soon as you think the wheather is fit for travalling. Thare is a

home here for him. My Mother and Maryann are vary wishfull he
Should come. As for my Self I will do all I can for him. He has had a
good aducation and he will be a great assistence to me. I have a good
deal of writing and corrospondence and he can assist me to manage the
business. I know you and Maryann will not like to part with him but
you will have the Satisfaction of knowing he is comming to a home with
his grandmother aunt and uncle.

I hope you are all ingoying good health. We are all quite well except
Maryann. She has been vary bad with bronchitis but She is mutch better at presant. The coal Strike is Settled over here and I hope 1894 will
be mutch more prosperious than 1893. I hope you have had a vary
happy Crismass and I wish you and Maryann and all the family a happy
and prosperious new year.

I remain

your effectionate Brother

William Reynolds

Inclosed I send you my likeness.

35. *William Reynolds to Laurence Reynolds*

1 Dudley Place

Old Trafford

Manchester

Feb 27/ 94

Dear Brother —

I received your Letter in due time and would have answered it before
but I have been bedfast and not able to do anything for nearly 5 weeks
with the influenza. I have had a Doctor attending me all the time. I am
now comming round vary niceley but I am not good for vary mutch yet.
I hope with the help of God to get pretty Strong again Shortley So that
I will be able to attend to my business. The wheather is against me as it
is vary cold and wat. We ware vary glad to hear that yourself Maryann
and all the children ware in good health. I have nothing further to write

about James William. When the time comes for leaving home you will Send us all perticulers and we will meet him at Liverpool.

Maryann has not been well for Some time with bronchitis and She has been obliged to Stay from business from time to time. My mother is getting vary good health and She has got through the winter vary well, infact she is the Strongest of the three. You can tell Willie I have not forgot him.

I have nothing more of any importance I can write to you about, only the business went on vary well during my illness. The coal Strike made a tarrable mess of all trades and only reviving vary sloley. Trade is not at all as good as it should be but we hope to have a good Summer and the Ship Canal is now open. The people of Manchester expects great things from the canal. It is certain to be a great halp. And trade is expected to be vary mutch increased.

John and his wife retired from business only a short time. She was not Satisfide and thay have taken a Shop in the Same line of business. And thay are commencing life again. His wife is a comical Sort of a person and never Satisfide.

Dear Brother, I am writing this Letter in my bedroom and hope with Gods help to be Soon out of it again. Mother and Maryann Sends thair best love to Maryann yourself and all the familey.

> I remain
> your effectionate Brother
> William Reynolds

36. *James William Reynolds to Laurence Reynolds*

[*written on William Reynolds's business stationery*]

Spring Bank, Longsight   Manchester
Memo: Laurence F. Reynolds   July 3d 1894

Dear Father,

Tomorrow is the Fourth and I suppose you entend haveing a good time. Think of me when you are having it. I thought I would write and describe the works. This building here is on the back of the property. This small place on the left is the engine room and storehouse on the right is the stable. The next is the French cleaning place. That is what caused the fire as he has it separate from the rest. Now by this picture you can not see the dyeing or soap cleaning places. There is another building that covers more ground than this only it is not as high. Then there is what they call the stove. That is a drying place. Then there is the office and receiving office & sorting rooms. This large place. First floor is where all the goods are pressed. 2nd all piece goods and the 3d where the lace curtains are dryed. Now across the road he has a piece of land about as large as two lots where he has a shed for the wagons and other truck. This piece of land is bounded by a stream of water[56] and all the water used in the place comes from that and you see he saves a lot of money by it. This large building I should judge is about 15 × 35. So now you know how large it is. There are 35 people on the pay roll. Besides there is two girls in each of the stores. That makes 10 more.

The folks here have to[o] much of the swelled head. They are always cracking themselves up and saying what they have done & how well off they are and all this it would make you sick. Grandmother is all right. I like her the best of the lot allthough they treat me right and all that, still, I am not at home. I will stick it out though and see what is what. If it does not show up in a year 'you can look for me coming home then.' There is one thing I forgot to tell you allthough they told me not to. You will wonder why I dont say something about uncle John. I only seen him once. I [am] going to see him tomorrow. Uncle Wm & Aunt Mary Ann and him are at outs, have been for some time. It seems he was not hightoned enough or something. There are two sides to the story and I do not really know which to receive.

Now do not take anything hard at what I am saying because what is done can not be undone but I can assure you if I had the least idea of what this was I would still be laboring for the [*illegible*] and have a little life. You cannot imagine what I left when I left Chgo. Now for instance I get up at between 6–30 & 7 every morning and am driven out to Longsight. Then I dodge around there all day bossing the men & girls getting out work. Then they quit at six. I wait till the vans come in then

go up home. It is always between nine & half-past nine when I get there.
Then we have a lunch and talk about business till ten or a quarter after,
then it is to bed. Every day the same. On Sunday I get up and go to
Mass generally with Aunt or Uncle. Last Sunday was the first I went
alone and I would not have gone I guess only uncle is in Ireland, then I
come home and talk or read prayers for the old lady then dinner. Probably after that uncle and I would take a walk. Look at nobody, talk to
nobody. Go around a couple of woods, then come back to supper. Then
to church. Then home. Talk awhile, then to bed. That is my life. So far
I would just as leave be in the bridewell for six months. Well Dad I
guess you know the situation I am in now. I will endeavor to make the
best of it for your sake, so let it drop. I only wished to let you know a
thing or two. Regards to Mother Tom John Mary Willie.

Your loving son

Jim

37. *Mary Ann Reynolds to Mary Ann Reynolds (née Kavanagh)*

1 Dudley Place

Old Trafford

Manchester

Sept 29/94

My Dear Sister Mary Ann — and Family,

Youre letter of the 27 of October [*sic*] in due time. I was away from
home when it arived here. I was at the seasoid for a few weeks at Black-
pool. I feel much better since I came back.

Dear Sister, We are all very well, thank God. Mother complanes but
it is only old age. We are glad to heare that you are all in good health.
We know all that is going on in Chicago now with all J.W. letters and
papers. He is doing very well. Just as mery as ever, always in good spirits. Mother is delighted when he comes home at night. I am glad to
heare Laurence looks so well and young. I must get my picture taken
and send you. I think I will beat him because people will not have it that
I am as old as I am. William is much better in health, thank God.

We we are all glad over heare when the strikes was settled in Chicago.[57] It must have made things very bad all over. I hope trade will soon revive again. That fire was an awfule calamity, towns distroyed. We often think what an awfull place America is. You are not safe but it is so very larg it is not like this small iland. It would go in a small corner of it. Has aney of your family been up to Uncle Jons this summer to see the old folks how they are getting on. I am very glad Mary is getting stron[g] again and little Willie. I should think he is getting along fine. He must not forget granmother in his prayers. Every day one hale Mary for her for a happy death.

Dear Sister, We are getting busyer in our buisnes this week. I think it will keep up now until christmass. J.W. is getting into the work very well. It is quite a change for him. It is all fun over in Chicago but it is all work in this countray, Except we go for a few weeks in the sommer to the seasoid.

Dear Sister, Mother wishes to be remembered to you & William also. She is always talking about Laurence and you.

> With kind love to all
> your loving sister
> M. A. Reynolds

38. *William Reynolds to Laurence and Mary Ann Reynolds*

[*written on black-bordered stationery*]

> 1 Dudley Place
> Old Trafford
> Manchester
> March 13 – 1895

Dear Brother & Sister,

Maryann and I received your letters last Saturday and we ware very pleased and thank you very hearthly for your Kind Sympathy. It was the only real Sympathy we received Since Mother died. We thank all the family Tom — John — Mary — Willia[m] all for their good hearthed Sympathy.

Dear Laurence, we know you falt Mothers death extremely and we falt it. It was vary trying to us allthough She was a great age. Still at the last She went quicker than we expected. If it was possible for us to keep her living for a mutch longer time nothing in the world would have pleased us better. She received everything religion could do for [her], and She was well attended by the doctor & nurse.

She was allways praying from morning till night, that was the way She Spent the principle part of her time. She gave us menay a good advise in our time as She was vary far seen, even in business mattars, and gave us a great example of patience. Maryann was ill for about a week after the funeral but She is now mutch better and able to go to business for a few hours each day. We had Some good friends at the funeral, near friends Hughie and his Sister. Mr. & Mrs Masterson also Mr & Mrs Flannigan.

Mother died 11/30 Monday night Feb 11th. I went at once for Mrs Flannigan and boath came back at once and told me thay would go to London to assist us and Edward was quite broken down. Mrs Flannigan acted one of the best friends we mat with. She is one of the old Stock and we cannot forget her. All our friends were Kind and had great Sympathy for us all the people at St Wilfrids. And all the Shopkeepers in Stretford Road, even the people at old Trafford, put down thair blinds the day of the funeral and Several of the Shops on Stretford Road put up thair Shutters till the funeral past. James assisted in every way possible and we ware vary well pleased he was over here at the time. He was present to[o] when She died. Thare was Maryann Hughie James & myself ware at the bedside when She died. Mother had a great Love for James as he Seen a good deal of her Since he has been here. Up to 4 or 5 weeks before her death She did not show any great Signs of weekness. She used to tell us her time was getting Short but it was the very Severe frost, it took a [great] meney old people. She was quite prepared and resigned and even a day or two before She died She was Satisfied to accept the will of God. She had every care and attantion and everything that could be done was done for her. She deserved all and the one great objact of our lives was if it was in our power to make her happy.

I think James told you how John acted. He done Something that was unworthy of himself. It was a very discrasefull action in the presence of our Friends and Father Lynch.[58] When Mother was very ill he had to be Sent for and than he came with a growl on his face. Maryann and I asked him to bring his wife to the funeral but he Said She would not come for Father Lynch. But he had the worst action of all to act the day of the funeral. I had 4 coaches & Hearse ordered, ample room for double the number who ware at the funeral. Father Lynch John Maryann & myself in the first coach. When we arrived at the cemitary Father Lynch got out and than he said my wife has a coach and I am going home with my wife. You can imagine how we falt to receive this Stab when my Mother was gatting put down in the clay. A real brother would assist us and Say you must not bear all the expanse yourself, I am not Short of money and I will do my part. No, he never mentioned a copper. One would think that a Sister and brother who stood by the old home So well deserved better treatment. John is one of the meanest misers in this town. We forgive tham and we hope God will forgive tham.

I am Sorry I have [been] obliged to write so mutch about a brother. Maryann is going to Send you a Letter. With love and best wishes to all

I remain

your effectionate Brother

William

39. *Mary Ann Reynolds to Mary Ann Reynolds (née Kavanagh)*

[*written on black-bordered stationery*]

1 Dudley Place

Old Trafford

Apr 18th 1894 [*recte* 1895]

My Dear Sister & Brother and family,

I would have writton to you sooner but my health was very bad since mothers death. I am very much improved now, thank God, and able to go to the shop every day.

We still feel very lonley without mother. I feel it very much because I was with her the most. Nearley all the day was spent with her befor she died. William is getting round now. He took mothers death to heart very much. We thought that she should never leave us. We did not consider her age because she was always interrested in the work.

Dear Sister, James is getting on very well. He is a proper American. He cannot see aneything here Like America. I dont wonder at him. It is all work here. Not so gay as Chicago. We had a letter this morning from Unkle John O'Toole. He was very sory about mothers death. All his family are well and he says they are doing very well. I suppose he did not think we [k]new all about them from James William.

Dear Sister, The weather is very fine just now. Easter Sunday and all Easter week was like summer weather. James was saying if it was as fine in Chicago they would turn out in their very best but it is not so here. We were very busy befor Easter & we wair glad of it. We had so much slack time in the winter. We havnot seen John since the day mother was buried and we donot want to see him. I hardly know what to tell you. I know James will tell you every thing.

I was glad to see Marys riting. It was very good. She will a very good writer. Tell her I want a letter from herselfe. I am sure Willie is a good boy. His writing is very good. He must try and get up to Mary.

Dear Sister, The advertisment in the Chicago paper was very good. We are getting the Letters on the gravestone of mothers death soon. We will send you a coppy of it.

Dear Sister, I have nothing more to tell you this time. I will write oftner now that I am better in health. Hoping you and Laurence and all the family are in they [*the*] best of health With kind love from William and myselfe & James.

Your affectionate sister
Mary Ann

Added at end: William Reynolds to James William Reynolds

Dec 31, 95

Dear James,

I received your letter and I was glad to hear that your Father & mother and all the family ware ingoying good health. We are well at present, Your aunt and myself. And the old year finished up well. We have not been so busy but Still we have nothing to complain of.

Hughie & Sister Alice spent the Chrismass with us. We had a great meney Crissass greetings aspecialy from our friends in Ireland. John Reynolds the carrage builder of Mohill sent me a Box containing some bottles of JJ&S best wiskey. All the works are well. I expect[ed] another letter from you befor xmas but I suppose you had no time as the wheather has been very cold.

Were you nearly Scared about the War Cry.[59] Thare is great talk here and according to the English papers the Americans are allfully frightened to tackle John Bull. We dont belive all we read in the papers here as thay say thay Can Blow the Americans to Smithereens as thay have no navy or army. Send us Some papers with your Side of the question as we would like to understand Both Sides.

I will conclude this letter. Your aunt joins me in wishing your Father & mother and all the family a happy and prosperous New [Year] from

your effectionate uncle
William

40. *Mary Ann Reynolds to Mary Ann Reynolds (née Kavanagh)*

3, Clarence Road,
Victoria Park,
Longsight, Manchester.
April 7 1896

Dear Sister,

We Received your letter on 3 inst and was pleased to hear you ware all quite well as we are enjoyning the Same at presant, thank God.

Your Letter was quite diferant to the previous one I had from you. You Said you would give me a Royal welcome. I think their is a doubt about it. Dont Excuse youre house to me. If it will Suit, you it will Satisfie me. I have had to ruff it in my time as much as anyone. I thought a trip to america would Restore my health a little as I am not atall Strong and I would like to Keep as quiet as possible untill I Return back if God Spares me.

We were Surprised to hear James is out of work So long. He Said in his Letters he did not look for work, it was all one round of pleashure. I whish we could Say the Same here as it is all one round of work with us, Except when the Summer comes we take a holiday for a week or two. You Said in your letter that James left a good Situation to come to Manchester. I have just found one of your letters writton before James left home saying his prospects are not very bright here at present. That does not Say he had a very good Situation. He ought to make a Start at anything and not be particular, living in a fine City like chicago where their are 2 millions of people.

William often wishes he had his business in your City. I think you ought to bee pleased to have James back after 16 months. He Returned home in good health . He is a very Delicate young man and if he Stoped another winter in Manchester it is doubtfull if you would See him agane. Dr Kennedy told us he was very delicate. He Said he never Seen a more delicate young man. When he was taken ill he Sunk rapidlty, onley with grate care we pulled him through.

I am getting old and it is as much as I can do to Look after myselfe, and if anything happened to James you would blame us. He was not atall fit for our work. It is a gob more Suitable for an older and Experianced man. If James got a fortune he would not Like Manchester. Their was nothing worth Looking at, Everyting dull, no life, no gayiety, nothing to be compared with america, if he worked 6 years in a basement where there was only 2 inches of Space over the Side walk for the Steam to come out. William Showed him the celler. He has gone through as much as would Kill a few and he has plenty of work in him yet. So you can See hard work does not Kill people. William was 5 years in business for himselfe at James age. We thought when he Returned home he would make a start at once. I want to See what Chicatgo is Like and then I will be the better judge.

The weather is very nice here at presant. We have cominced today after the holidays. William would have answered James letter but he has not been so well for a month or two. He had Dr Kennedy atending him. He had influense [*influenza*] agane. He is nearley quite well now. We have been busy this Easter time.

I will Send you a Letter before I Start for newyork to Say the time I will arive in Chicago.

With Best wishes to all the family
Your affectionate Sister
Mary Ann

41. *Mary Ann Reynolds to Laurence and Mary Ann Reynolds*

3, Clarence Road,
Victoria Park,
Longsight,
Manchester.
July 28th 96

Dear Laurence, Mary ann and family,

Just a few Lines to Let you Know I have made My Mind up to visit America. I secured my berth on the umbria of the cunard line. Will Sail from Liverpool on agust 8th and is Expected to arrive at Newyork agust 15th. I hope the voyage will do my health good. I expect Cousin Thomas Reynolds will Meet Me when the Ship arrives at Newyork. I have received Several Letters from him. He has given me great incouragment to Cross the atlantic. Nothing would please him and his family better than to See me. If all is well I will Spend a few days in Newyork before Starting for Chicago. William is wishfull for me to get back as Soon as possible. He thinks I can do it in 6 weeks. I Know he will feel my absence very much. But he does not mind that if the voyage will do me good. If I dont feel able for all the Jurney to Chicago and Uncle Johns I will stay at Newyork and That is If I dont feel Strong when I get to NewYork. If I feel able to do all the Jurney I will divide the time between the 3 places. I will Send you a Talagram when I am going to take train from Newyork.

William and Myself are enjoying very good health at presant, thank god. I hope this Letter will find you all in the very best of health. We have had a very hot Summer in England this time, Somthing Like America. We have a chang this week, it has gon much colder, the weather doesnot Let us have much light cloathes here. We have been very Busy this Sason.

William had a holiday in the Isle of Man. It is a very nice place. It don him a Lot of Good. I hope and trust in god I will Return back to old England better and Stronger.

I have nothing more particular to tell you. I will bring all the news I can with me and we can talk it over.

> With Love and Best wishes from William and Myselfe
> Youre Affectionate Sister
> Mary Ann Reynolds

42. *William Reynolds to Laurence Reynolds and James William Reynolds*

> 3 Clarence Road
> Longsight
> Manchester
> Jan 1/98

Dear Laurence,

I received James's Letter this morning and Maryann and myself were glad to hear that you whare recovering from your long illness. We were very uneasy till we got the letter. James did not Say in his letter what you complained of. It must have been a very trying illness whitch brought you down so much as Maryann told me you were very Strong when she left Chicago. And we hope and trust in God in your next letter we will hear of your quite recovery.

Dear James, We were glad to hear that you were working and have a prospect of a good post in time. You did not mention anything of your Mother or the remainder of the family. We hope thay are all ingoying good health. We received a letter this morning from Mr Tom Reynolds Doughter (She is in a convent home on the Hudson) informing us that she had taken the vows of the order of St Vincent. She is a full nun and quite happy. We hear very often from Uncle Johns family as Frank Send us two papers every Week. And thay are all in good health at present. Hughie and his Sister and Brothers are getting good health and doing very well, have 2 Shops Now, have taken Johns other shop in Brook St. John has retired again but Still not Satisfied, he is like a Duck out of water. I suppose he will have another try soon again. We were pleased to hear that P J Reynolds was getting on well Kindley remember Maryann to Father Reynolds the first time you See him. Maryann is getting pretty good health. She has got through the winter So far very nicely. The winter has been very mild, no frost or snow yet. I have got good health. During 1897 I have had no illness. I have been very moderate in my drinks and I have given up Basss ale alltogather, it was to[o] strong. I had my holiday in the Isle of Man and Ireland. You know McCardell, him and I went togather. We went first to Douglas for a few days and Sailed from thare to Belfast and went on to Ballameney. It is a nice country. Stayed two days thare, drove all round. Thare is no poor people, all comfortable. It is the Linan Centre. Came on to Portrush and the Giants Causway and than returned to Belfast, went on to Dublin and returned to the Isle of Man. McCardell is very nice to travvall with. One half a glass of wine in two days effected his head. The trip improved my health very much.

You will be Supprised to hear that I have commenced in the Laundry business about 9 months ago. I have Sunk about £400 in machinery. One machine cost £200. The goods are brought from the Hydro and dried and finished as fast as thay are put through. I have all the same workpeople I had when you were here. I get all the washing from the Albion Hotel whitch comes to about £20 per month and I do the washing for the Wallington Hotel also. I think it will be a good thing in time but will want more machinery and more hands. I will Send you more perticulars in my letter. Maryann joins me in wishing your Father and your Mother yourself and all the family a Very Happy and prosperous New Year.

I remain

your effectionate uncle

William Reynolds

write Soon

43. *William Reynolds to James William Reynolds*

3 Clarence Road

Victoria Park

Longsight

Manchester

Feb 21/98

Dear James,

I received your letter and Maryann & myself were glad to hear that your Father had improved So well and we hope the improvement will continue till he is quite Strong again. Also glad to hear that all the family are getting on So well.

Thare are a great meney people comming from the States this year visiting Ireland in honor of the centenary of 98.[60] If your Father got sufficentley strong I think the voyage across the water would do him good and might be the means of building his health up again.

The Irish fair[61] in Chicago was a great success and must have caused a great deal of pleasure with having the Soil from the different countys. I feel sure the people must have been delited. We received a letter from Francis about Uncle Johns Golden Jubilee in March next and that all the family were quite well and expected thair Son William and other children to be with tham at thair Jubilee. Maryann speaks of Aunt most highly, been [*being*] good hearted and a very kind woman. She Ses She can never forget her kindness to her during her visit.

Thare is going to be a Grand Ball in Manchester St Patrick's night for the benifit of the distress in Ireland.[62] A committee of Ladies both English and Irish has been formed for the purpose. I intend to be present. I don't know wheather you have heard of the fund that it has been formed here for the same purpose. Up to the present thare has been Subscribed £50–0–0 and the fund is Still increasing and will be kept open for Some time.

Hughie and all the family are quite well and working the sime as usuel. Your Uncle John is taking it easy, still living retired. Maryann is getting pretty good health considering it is winter. She has her old complaint Bronctitos but she still goes to Stretford Road Shop each day. The winter has been very mild here. My own health is allright. I have nothing to complain of except Sometimes I feel I get rather too much work to do. I have to Stick Very close to it, more espicely now with having the Laundry attached. It is going on as well as I expected. We receive everything for washing, all done by Machinary. I have a new machine by power and heated by gas for Ironing collars cuffs and fronts. It is a very usefull machine and Irons the things very rapidely.

Inclosed I send you postal order for £5/, £3 for your Father & £2 for yourself, hoping the next letter we receive from you we will have further good news of your Fathers health still improving.

Maryann joins me in Sending our love and best wishes to Father Mother and all the family.

I remain
your affectionate Uncle
William Reynolds

44. *William Reynolds to James William Reynolds*

> 3 Clarence Road
> Victoria Park
> Longsight
> Manchester
> May 2 98

Dear James,

I received your letter dated April 20th and also your previous letter and would have sent you letter before but I was waiting for the letter you promised. Maryann and myself were very upset and grieved to hear of your Fathers death. We did not expect he would have died so quickley. We had hopes of his reovery when he got over the most trying part of his illness but the worst thing we considered was getting so reduced. What seemed to us the worst feature of his terriable illness. I did live in the hopes of seeing him sometime either in Chicago or in Manchester myself.

John was very sorry to hear of his death, also Hughie, Alice and all the family. Maryann had masses offered for his recovery. One mass was on the morning of April 20th and since we received your letter your last letter we had masses offered up for his soul. I am sure your Mother felt his loss most extremely and all the family as he was a very good Father. All his thoughts and cares were always centered in his family as all his letters to us were always informing us how the children were getting on His family seemed to be all his delight and study and I am sure you will all mis him very much but as it was Gods will to take him you must all feel reconsiled as we do not know how soon it may come to our own turn. We were pleased to hear he had some good friends at his bed side when he died. Father Reynolds and his brother Mr P J Reynolds Mary Ann and myself symthyise with your Mother and all the family in your sad bereaveiment.

> I remain
> your affactionate uncle
> William Reynolds

Write soon and kindley remember your Aunt Mary Ann to Father Reynolds.

45. *William Reynolds to William Patrick Reynolds* [63]

281 Regent Road
Dec 2/98

My Dear Young Nephew,

I received your letter and I was vary glad to See you ware getting on So well at School. I would advise you to attand Strictley to your Books for now is the time and when you get to be a young man you will find the great Benifit of Looking well to your Books. And you will be Better able to assist your Mother and Father. In Concludesion Dear William I want you to Say 3 hail Marys for me once only. And whan you are all round your Table cristmass eve Sing a little Song in rememberence of your uncle

William

46. *Mary Ann Reynolds to Mary Reynolds Jr* [64]

1, Norton Place,
Wilmslow Road,
Fallowfield.
Manchester
Nov 4/00

My Dear Niece,

I received your letter and portrait in due time. I was pleased to get your first letter. After all these years. You look well. Your Uncle is very pleased with your likness. He Says you are quite a yong lady.

You are going in for plenty of learning. I hope you will Succeed. I think their is every prospect of you Succeding. We are pleased to hear that your Mother and all our nephews are enjoying good health.

We are both in good halth. Your Uncle gets the best of health last 18 monthes. You will See by the heading of this letter we removed from our last house 19 monthes ago. It was very damp and we were loosing our health in it. We are quite in the countrary [*country*].

Our house is twice as larg as the last one. We have a larg garden at the back, plenty of appltrees and curran[t] bushes & cherries. We just put a lot of apples away for the winter. Our house fronts the high road with a large flower garden in front. I think James will know wher it is. It has a very plesant view.

We have been busy, considering the Slackness in trade at presant. Every thing has advanced in price. Coale & spirrets has gon up more than double the price on acount of the war.[65] England will pay dear for it. John Bull is never Satisfyd. He must be fighting but he has suffered this time in the great loss of lives and a great maney more lives will be lost befor all is setted.

I am pleased to hear that Father Reynolds takes a great intrest in the family. Kindley Remember me to him. William would like to get a letter from James to let him know how he is getting on. And if he is thinking of getting married. He must not take his Uncles example or he will left on the shelf. Now Dear niece I think I have told you all I could think of.

> With kind love to all
> I remane
> Youre affectionate Aunt
> Mary A. Reynolds

47. *William Reynolds to James William Reynolds*

> 1, Norton Place
> Wilmslow Road,
> Fallowfield.
> Jan 18 – 1901

Dear James,

I received your letter Saturday evening Jan 5th and Maryann and myself were very pleased to hear from you. I felt proud you got a position with the ice Co. You Seem to have a very responsiable post and I think it will Suit you if your Selery is equel to the amount of work you have to contend with.

Maryann and Myself were pleased to hear that you were all injoying good health, your Mother, Tom, John, Mary and Willie. We were so pleased we drank a bottle of champagne. So I guess we drank your health.

Dear James, I will now tell you a few perticulers about myself and the business. I have got on very well considering. The Year 1898 was a record year for me but 99 went down through the war. Coal and Spirit advanced double. I think this year will be better commincing the New Century. The Laundry is going on pretty well. I lost Some of the old workers, Ferguson and Woolford. I still have Martin and he is now the Foreman. He has turned out a good man. I have Dan also. He is a good man. Mathue Park is also with me and nearly all the other workers.

The building I have had built is between the shed and the railway line. I purchased the land from the Canons. Between the works and the railway line thare is over 2000 yards. The building is on the bottom po[r]tion near the brook. It is a good building, 3 Storyes & 91 feet long. I am going to Let off to Tennants. Mr Williams the grocer Dickinson Road is taking half 12 Stalls for his horses. A Bill posting Co has taking the Side facing the Railway, 600 square yds of Brick work without windows. What do you think about this spec. I was paying chief rent £24 per year for 3 years and never received one penny, So I was obliged to do Something. You can See I have not been idle. I never worked so hard in my life as I did last year all through the war. If I have good luck with the building it will be one of the best investments I have made. My health has been very good Since we went to live in Fallowfield. Mary Ann has had much better health. Our house is fine, by far the best house we have lived in yet and it is quite a treat to get home at night. All the shops are doing well. Stockport Shop has not been opened So long, So it is doing as well as we could expect.

Your Uncle John has retired. He is walking about now trying to kill time. Hughie and all the family are doing well. Hughie & Owen went to Ireland and brought two wifes back last Nov. 1900. By all appearances The Reynoldss will not die out in Manchester.

Dear James, Dont think that we will forget you as thare are none nearer to us than Laurences family. We were delited with Mary. She got on So well at school.

The new building will cost me between 7 & 8 hundred pounds. I bought 5 houses of Slade Lane for Maryann about 2 years ago and paid £1000 pounds for tham She has tham in her own right and receives an income of £2 per week from tham. Her living is now I think secure.

I have been cycling for about 3 years. I find it very usefull to going to business. I can get home in about a ¼ of an hour and it saves me a great deal of time. I have had much better health Since I have commenced 12 months.

Last Summer McCardell and I went to Bray. We Stayed at old Mrs Barrows. We both had Bikes and we went over the Sugar Loaf Mountains on to the ruin of the 7 Churches. We had a fine time and injoyed ourselves much. I am Sure you will get tired reading this letter.

I met Sargent Gill the other day and he made great inquires about you. He sas dont forget to mention my name the next time you write. He Said I did admire that young man. He Said I am Sure he will get on well and make his mark. I will Send you more information in my next letter. I am very busy at present having the finishing touches to the new building.

Mary Ann joins me in Sending our best wishes to all the family. Remember us to Father Reynolds.

I remain
your affectionate Uncle
William Reynolds

P.S. I think with help of God I might be able to visit Chicago Sometime. I know the Sail across the Atlantic would do me good. I am sorry I have not been able to answer your letter sooner. Write soon.

WR

48. *Mary Ann Reynolds to Mary Reynolds Jr*

1, Norton Place,
Wilmslow Road,
Fallowfield.
Manchester
March 27/001

My Dear Niece,

I rceived youre Kind letter of January 21st and was glad to heare you ware all well. I would have answered it Sooner but I have not been well Sence this year Set in. Some weeks not able to go out. We have had very bad weather and a great dale of Sickness in Manchester. Nearley every person was complaning about the weather, nasty damp cold weather, nasty damp cold weather.

Your Uncle William is in the best of health. He got all the papers and James letter. He will write Soon. He is very busy at presant. We are always busy befor Easter.

Dear Mary, I am Proud to hear you Love the old Land sow well. The war in South Africa is nearly settled. It will be a good thing for both Sids. England has lost the best men in her army and it Servs her jolley well Right. We will have to suffer paying tax.

I was Sorry abot Father Reynolds brother getting hurt sow badley. I hope he is quite well by this time. Remember Me to Father Reynolds. He is a fine Irish Man.

We read all the papers. The ware fine. I get 2 Every week. The Milwakee Citize[n], a very good catholic paper. The other is the Darlington Democrat. Sow you See I have a lot of american news.

My Dear Niece, By the time you get this letter we will be near the Great feast of Easter. Enclosed is an Easter Card. I would like a better one but today it was Sow Cold to go far. It was Snowing fast this afternoone.

Now I finish Wishing you all Mother yourselfe & all my nephews a joyouse Easter.

Your Sincere Aunt
Mary A. Reynolds

PS Youre Uncle John is in good health and his wife. I dont think he will start in buisness again. He has anough to Keep them.

49. *William Reynolds to James William Reynolds*

> 1, Norton Place,
> Wilmslow Road,
> Fallowfield.
> Aug 13/01

Dear James,

I received your letter in due time and I am Sorry I have not been able to Send you an answer Sooner. I hope your mother and all the family are quite well, yourself included. We read in the newspapers the acount of the great heat in Chicago and other places in America. It was Something extreme. I hope all your family pulled through allright. This has been the hottest Summer in Manchester for 50 years. We had the heat wave but nothing like you had it in Chicago. It was nearly 90 in the Shade.

Everything is going on about the Same in Manchester except trade is very quite [*quiet*]. The Boar War has ruined a lot of people. England was in a prosperous State when the war commenced but everything is changed and the prices of allmost everything has advanced from about 25 to 50 per cent. Coal advanced over 100 per cent. Within the last few months it has come down. Petroleum spirit advanced over 100 percent. America aught to be doing well. I seen in the papers that trade is very good in the States. Let me know if you are doing well in the new position you got. Kindley Send word if all the family are getting on well. Thare has been no money made Since the war commenced.

Hughie and all his family are going on about the Same. Your Aunt Maryann is getting good health. She has gust returned from her holiday in Ireland. As far as health is conserened I have nothing to complain of. I have had much better health Since we have gone to Fallowfield. Your uncle John is walking about as usual, has not done any work for about 4 years. The warehouse I had built on the vacant land is going on well.

I got 3 good tenants and it has turned out very well. I received £92 per year from the tennants whitch will help to meet Some of extre expence. I have nearly all the old workers in my imploy yet. I will Send you more perticulers in my next letter.

Kindley remember your Aunt and myself to Father Reynolds and all the friends in Chicago. I send my best wishes to your Mother and all the family.

I remain
your Effectionate Uncle
William Reynolds

p.s. Write Soon and Send all perticulers.

50. *William Reynolds to James Wiliam Reynolds*

[*written on black-bordered stationery*]

293 Wilmslow Road
Fallowfield
Manchester
April 19th 1904

Dear James,

I received your letter sympathising with me in the great loss I have sustained in the death of your Aunt Mary Ann. It was the heaviest blow I have received during all my life and it came so sudden and unexpected. We were both enjoying good health up to the commencement of March and we talked together how we had got over the winter so well. I caught a cold first and an attack of neuralgia. Of course she had her old complaint Bronchitis every winter but as far as I could see she seemed to have got over this winter better than any for the last 5 years and showed no sign of anything unusual till about the 15th of March. On the 16th of March she went out to do a little shopping and was out for about half-an-hour but during the time she was out the east wind caught her severely and caused a pain in her back. When I went to dinner she was complaining of the pain and said the cold had caught her. The Doctor was called to the house at the time to see her and came in at dinner time while I was presant and did not think there was anything unusual but said she would be all right in a day or two. She seemed to get a little worse but did not take to her bed until Friday. She then commenced to cough rather bad and on Saturday she got rather downcast, a thing I never saw before in my life as she was a woman with a splendid spirit. When I saw this change it began to effect me very much. It seemed to completily get over my feelings. Saturday night she had a bad night and I went into her bedroom during the night several times She had a friend sleeping in there. I saw the way she was breathing and thought she could not possibly last very long but as morning advanced she seemed to recover her breathing. I went off early in the morning and got the Doctor out of bed to come to see her. He still thought she would be right in a day or two and the Priest also thought the same.

About 6 oclock on Sunday evening she took a change for the worse as she coughed very bad during the day and became unconscious. I brought the Doctor quickly again and a specialist to consult with him. After consulting together they told me that if she did recover she would be part paralyzed but she never recovered and died next morning at 15 past 6. It was a terrible blow to me and I ill at the time myself. I thought I should never have got over it. The Doctor fully expected to see me laid up. I could not comprehend it, her dying so quickly and her & I being together all our lives. The last 5 years especially was the most pleasant time we had during our lives as we had a fine house to live in in a nice locality and enjoyed the home better than anything we had before.

I thank your Mother Tom John Mary & Willie for their sympathy with me in my great distress. I sent you papers about the funeral which I supposed you received.

I am now beginning to get over the feeling of distress a little but dont expect ever to be the same again as I am getting advanced in years.

I remain
Your affectionate Uncle
William Reynolds

Abbreviations

HCP House of Commons Papers
NAI National Archives, Dublin
NLI National Library of Ireland, Dublin

Notes to Introduction

1 The pessimistic tone for Manchester's history was established with the publication of the *Report on the State of the Irish Poor in Great Britain*, HCP, 1836 (40), xxxiv, 427. See also the *District Committee Reports of the Manchester and Salford Sanitary Association, 1853–4*, and the Association's published tracts and lectures, 1853–4, in the Manchester Central Library, Archives, M126/15/nos 1–105. Friedrich Engels drew on Manchester for evidence in his classic polemic of 1845, *The Condition of the Working-Class in England* (English translation, London, 1892).

2 Modern research work on Manchester began with Asa Briggs's *Victorian Cities* (London, 1968). Revisionist studies of the Irish experience in Manchester were published in Roger Swift and Sheridan Gilley (eds), *The Irish in the Victorian City* (London, 1985) and in W. J. Lowe, *The Irish in Mid-Victorian Lancashire: The Shaping of a Working-Class Community* (New York, 1989). Recently Mervyn Busteed has continued the revision with ' "The Most Horrible Spot"? The Legend of Manchester's "Little Ireland" ', *Irish Studies Review*, no. 13 (winter 1995–96), pp. 12–20, and 'The Myth and Reality of Irish Migrants in Mid-Nineteenth-Century Manchester' in Patrick O'Sullivan (ed.), *The Irish World Wide: History, Heritage, Identity*, ii: *The Irish in the New Communities* (London & Leicester, 1992). The most recent survey of Manchester is Alan Kidd, *Manchester* (Keele, 1996).

3 Problems stemming from the lack of first-person accounts pertaining to the social history of Lancashire are noted by Bernard Aspinwall, *Arrival, Assertion and Acclimatisation, or Context and Contrasts: A Preliminary Checklist of Works on the Irish Catholic Experience in the Northwest of England* (Wigan, 1996), pp. 8–10.

4 Registers for Parish of Mohill, Diocese of Ardagh and Clonmacnois: NLI, p. 4239. The register does not include marriages, baptisms or burials before 1836. Reynolds family records indicate that Patrick Reynolds was born in 1809 and that Mary O'Toole was born in 1810.

5 Tithe Composition Book for the Parish of Mohill, 1834: Corrig, p. 23: NAI, TAB/16/16.

6 Field Book: County of Leitrim, Barony of Mohill, Parish of Mohill, 1838, p. 146: General Valuation Office, Dublin.

7   Ordnance Survey Map (1851): County Leitrim, Union of Mohill. The area was surveyed in 1837. Carrick is located on sheet 33.

8   For descriptions of Mohill's agricultural produce and marketing procedures see the land valuator's opening remarks in the Field Book (see n. 6). See also *Returns of Agricultural Produce in Ireland, in the year 1847*, pt I, HCP, 1847–48 [923], lvii, 1, pp. 62–3; pt II. HCP, 1847–48 [1000], lvii, 109, pp. 8–9; *Return showing the Amount of Prices of Agricultural Produce of Forty Towns in Ireland during the years 1848, 1850 and 1851*, HCP, 1852 [307], xlvii, 7.

9   National Schools Register, County Series: Co. Leitrim, Vol. 1: Mohill, pp. 1–8: NAI, ED/2/25.

10 The parochial register for Mohill shows a death notice for a Patrick Reynolds on 2 March 1848; Reynolds family tradition, however, places Patrick's death date in 1849.

11 Lowe, *The Irish in Mid-Victorian Lancashire*, ch. 2 'The Famine Immigration', pp. 21–44.

12 For the earliest indication of a transfer of Patrick Reynolds's land see *General Valuation of Rateable Property in Ireland: Valuation of the Several Tenements Comprised in the Union of Mohill, in the County of Leitrim* [Griffith's Valuation] (Dublin, 1857), p. 126; Revision Book, 1860–94: Rural District of Mohill, Electoral Division of Mohill, p. 7: General Valuation Office, Dublin.

13 Ruth-Ann Harris, *The Nearest Place That Wasn't Ireland: Early Nineteenth-Century Irish Labor Migration* (Ames, Iowa, 1994), pp. 92, 125–7.

14 Lowe, *The Irish in Mid-Victorian Lancashire*, p. 47, places the number of Irish-born people living in Manchester/Salford in 1851 at approximately 53,000.

15 Many of the census enumerators' pages for Manchester in 1851 were destroyed in a flood. A search for the family in the Salford and Liverpool census returns for 1851 also proved fruitless.

16 The Ordnance Survey Map for Manchester (1849), sheet 34, incorrectly identifies Buxton Street in Chorlton-upon-Medlock as Burton Street. For descriptions of the area see Busteed, '"The Most Horrible Spot"?'; M. A. Busteed, R. I. Hodgson and T. F. Kennedy, 'The Myth and Reality of Irish Migrants in Mid-Nineteenth-Century Manchester' in O'Sullivan (ed.), *The Irish World Wide*, ii, 26–51.

17 Michael Anderson, *Family Structure in Nineteenth-Century Lancashire* (Cambridge, 1971), pp. 41–2.

18 John Hatton, 'A Lecture on the Sanitary Condition of Chorlton-upon-Medlock', 12 Jan. 1854: Manchester Central Library, Manuscripts and Archives, M126/5/1/17. For the visitors' description of Buxton Street see ibid., M126/2/4/8. The Sanitary Association published dozens of pamphlets, including: *Notice to the Working Classes on Lime Washing to Prevent Diseases*; *Hints to Working People about the Houses They Live In*; *The Physical and Moral Evils Arising from Weather,*

Heat, Cold, Damp, Want of Light, Cellar and Court Residences, etc.; and *Co-operation and the Social Duties of Man.*

19 'Memoir of Brother Ignatius of the Xaverian Institute', *The Harvest: An Organ of Catholic Works*, x, no. 118 (July 1897), pp. 148–50. For a comprehensive treatment of education in the city see David Lannon, 'Bishop Turner and Educational Provision within the Salford Diocesan Area, 1840–1870' (M.Phil. thesis, University of Hull, 1994).

20 George Wright & Sons, located in Chorlton-upon-Medlock, was one of Manchester's largest dyeworks.

21 Paul Johnson, *Saving and Spending: The Working-Class Economy in Britain, 1870–1939* (Oxford, 1985), pp. 7–8.

22 The execution of the 'Manchester Martyrs' and the attraction of Lancashire's Irish emigrants to the revolutionary movement of Fenianism is discussed in Lowe, *The Irish in Mid-Victorian Lancashire*, pp. 189–98.

23 Anderson, *Family Structure*, ch. 6: 'Aspects of Relationships within the Urban Nuclear Family', pp. 68–78.

24 The Reynolds letters provide some striking comparisons and contrasts between conditions facing first-generation emigrant families in Chicago and Manchester. Laurence and his wife were in fact successful parents; their children graduated from high school and entered professions. Their daughter Mary, for example, became a public school principal, and their son Tom became a dentist. The best overview of Irish emigration to the United States is Lawrence J. McCaffrey's *The Irish Diaspora in America* (Washington DC, 1984).

25 'A Short History of the ASD', Part 1 (Bradford: Amalgamated Society of Dyers, Bulletin no. 2 (1979)), pp. 1–2: typescript in the Working Class Movement Library, Salford. See also Walter Bateson, *The Way We Came: An Historical Retrospect of the Adventures of the Pioneers of the Amalgamated Society of Dyers* (Bradford, 1928). Bateson notes (pp. 8–9) that the hard work and low wages did not attract the best calibre of workmen and that dyers were looked upon as non-skilled and among the lowest class of labourers.

26 Minute Book of the Bleachers' and Dyers' Mutual Indemnity Company, Limited, from 1898: Greater Manchester County Record Office, G14/14/1/1.

27 This journal first appeared in August 1881 as *The Dyer: The Representative Journal of the Dyers, Cleaners, Bleachers, Drysalters, Colour Makers, Soap and Chemical Manufactures, and Allied Trades.*

28 Johnson, *Saving and Spending*, p. 5.

29 Rev. P. Laurence O'Toole, *History of the Clan O'Toole* (Dublin, 1890).

30 Steven Fielding, 'Irish Politics in Manchester, 1890–1914', *International Review of Social History*, xxxiii (1988), pp. 261–84.

31   Steven Fielding, *Class and Ethnicity: Irish Catholics in England, 1880–1939* (Buck-
      ingham, 1993), ch. 5: 'The Politics of Home Rule', pp. 79–104. See also J. Dun-
      leavy, 'The Irish Dimension of the British Labour Movement, 1886–1929', *North
      West Labour History*, no. 15 (1990–91), pp. 59–66.

Notes to Narrative

1   Baltimore and Ohio Rail Road workers were on strike in Chicago and across the
     country in 1877.
2   Disraeli sent the British fleet and Indian troops to the eastern Medititerranean
     region when hostilities broke out in 1878 between Russia and Turkey.
3   Pope Pius IX (1792–1878; reign, 1846–78).
4   Mary is referring to her brother, John O'Toole, in Schullsburg, Wisconsin.
5   Mary is referring to her brother, William O'Toole, in Carrick, Annaduff, Co.
     Leitrim.
6   Cecily was Mary Reynolds's sister.
7   Charles Stewart Parnell (1846–91), chairman of the Irish Parliamentary Party;
     John Dillon (1851–1927), a leading member of the party.
8   Cartes-de-visite, small photographic portraits mounted on cards measuring 3½in.
     × 2½in., the equivalent of modern passport photographs.
9   Violence during the Land War reached a high point in August in Co. Mayo with
     the assassination of David Feerick, an agent of a local landlord, George Browne.
10   Mary Ann and her sister-in-law in Chicago referred to one another as 'sister'.
11   The *Salford Weekly News*, 5 Feb. 1881, carried the story of the expulsion of thirty-
     six members of the Irish Parliamentary Party from the House of Commons on 3
     February.
12   Michael Davitt (1846–1906), member of the Irish Parliamentary Party, was
     arrested in Dublin.
13   The *Manchester Evening News*, 10 Feb. 1881, reported that 4,000 people attended
     the meeting at the Free Trade Hall.
14   A. M. Sullivan (1830–84), member of the Irish Parliamentary Party.
15   Newspaper reports of the bombing appeared on 15 January 1881. Detectives the-
     orised that the bomb was either placed inside by an Irish soldier serving in one of
     the regiments or by Fenians.
16   Knock, Co. Mayo, became a pilgrimage site after 21 August 1879, when an
     apparition of the Virgin Mary, St Joseph, and St John the Evangelist was reported
     by several local residents.

17 James Curran was a family friend who emigrated from Manchester to the United States; he returned frequently to Manchester but ultimately retired in the United States.

18 William is referring to the government's attempt to suppress the Land League through the arrest and imprisonment of Parnell and other members of the Irish Party in the autumn of 1881.

19 Mary Ann Reynolds, who had broken her leg, gave birth to her only daughter, Mary.

20 Anna Parnell (1852–1911), sister of Charles Stewart Parnell and founder of the Ladies' Land League in 1881. She spoke in Manchester on 23 January 1882 to a crowd of nearly 5,000.

21 Mary is employing the nickname Irish nationalists used to refer to W. E. Forster (1818–86), who was then Chief Secretary for Ireland.

22 Parnell issued the No Rent Manifesto in October 1881.

23 The prominence given to Irish affairs in the English press at this time was largely due to the public concern arising from the Phoenix Park murders of 6 May 1882, when the newly appointed Chief Secretary for Ireland, Lord Frederick Cavendish, and his Under-Secretary, T. H. Burke, were assassinated in Dublin by members of a secret society known as the 'Invincibles'.

24 Walter Bourke and his soldier bodyguard were shot to death in Gort, Co. Galway, on 8 June 1882.

25 The exhibition was scheduled for Dublin to showcase native industries and businesses.

26 Leaders of the Irish Parliamentary Party met in Leeds on 29 September 1882 with approximately 100 representatives of Land and Labour League branches in England to reorganise them into the Irish National League of Great Britain.

27 T. P. O'Connor (1848–1929), Irish Parliamentary Party member who sat for the Scotland Division of Liverpool after 1885.

28 Thomas Sexton (1848–1932), a leading member of the Irish Parliamentary Party.

29 Salford's nationalists belonged to the John Dillon Branch of the Irish Land League of Great Britain.

30 Cabinet photographs measured 6½ in. × 4¼ in., i.e. about twice the size of cartes-de-visite (see n. 8).

31 The great storm occurred on 11–12 December 1883.

32 Meetings in favour of Home Rule for Ireland were held in several American cities when the Liberal government introduced the first Home Rule Bill.

33 An earthquake struck Charlestown, South Carolina, on 31 August 1886, killing eighty people and damaging ninety per cent of the buildings.

34 Construction of the Manchester Ship Canal began in 1887 and was completed in 1894.

35   The Royal Jubilee Exhibition was held in Manchester during the summer of 1887.

36   William F. Cody (1846–1917), also known as 'Buffalo Bill', was a hunter and showman.

37   Arthur Balfour (1848–1930), Chief Secretary for Ireland, had introduced a series of coercion acts to suppress agrarian outrages.

38   Benjamin Harrison (1833–1901) was elected President of the United States in November, 1888.

39   President Grover Cleveland sent Sir Lionel Sackville-West back to England after the publication of the ambassador's opinionated correspondence, which was seen to be interfering in the United States election of 1888.

40   The infamous 'Jack the Ripper' was committing his series of murders in 1888–89.

41   Michael O'Toole was William's great-uncle from Aghintass, Annaduff, Co. Leitrim. Letter taken from a draft in William's letter-book.

42   The McGushans were family friends from Drumod Beg, Annaduff, Co. Leitrim.

43   Rev. Francis L. Reynolds served Laurence Reynolds's family in St Anne's parish, Chicago.

44   William is responding to the news that Chicago would stage the Columbian Exposition, the first 'world's fair', in 1893.

45   Parnell was named co-respondent in the divorce case between Katharine O'Shea (1845–1921) and William O'Shea (1840–1905), a former member of the Irish Parliamentary Party.

46   William O'Brien (1852–1928), a leading member of the Irish Parliamentary Party.

47   William E. Gladstone (1809–98), the Liberal Party leader and Prime Minister.

48   Several leading members of the Irish Parliamentary Party were touring the United States when Parnell was ousted as chairman of the party.

49   Very Rev. Canon Patrick O'Toole (1807–92), of St Wilfrid's parish, was the most respected priest in Manchester.

50   William is referring to the massacre of approximately 200 Sioux at Wounded Knee, South Dakota, by United States cavalry on 29 December 1890.

51   Mary Reynolds lived in Carrick, Mohill, Co. Leitrim.

52   Mary Ann is referring to Hugh Reynolds, who remained in Manchester as a life-long friend of William. He died around 1932.

53   Robert O'Brien, solicitor, Mohill, Co. Leitrim.

54   Rev. Patrick Daly (1857–1910) served in St Joseph's parish, Longsight.

55   William is referring to the rejection of the second Home Rule Bill by the House of Lords.

56   James is referring to Gore Brook.

57   Mary Ann is referring to the famous Pullman strike in 1894.

58 Rev. P. Lynch served in St Wilfrid's parish, Manchester.

59 The United States government invoked the Monroe Doctrine in 1895 to press Britain to settle a longstanding boundary dispute between Venezuela and British Guiana.

60 Irish nationalists celebrated the centennial of the rebellion of 1798.

61 An Irish Fair was held in Chicago on 6 December 1897 to raise funds to construct a monument in honour of the Irish patriot Robert Emmet.

62 Funds were collected to provide relief for victims of famine in the congested districts of the west of Ireland.

63 William Patrick Reynolds, Laurence's and Mary Ann's youngest son.

64 Mary Reynolds, Laurence's and Mary Ann's daughter (also the recipient of Letter 48).

65 The South African War (1899–1902).

Bibliography

Amalgamated Society of Dyers, 'Research Notes on the History of the National Union of Dyers, Bleachers and Textile Workers', Bulletin no. 1 (July 1979) (typescript in the Working Class Movement Library, Salford)

'A Short History of the ASD', Part 1, Bulletin no. 2 (1979); Part 2, Bulletin no. 3 (1980) (typescript in the Working Class Movement Library, Salford)

Anderson, Michael, *Family Structure in Nineteenth-Century Lancashire* (Cambridge, 1971)

Aspinwall, Bernard, *Arrival, Assertion and Acclimatisation, or Context and Contrasts: A Preliminary Checklist of Works on the Irish Catholic Experience in the Northwest of England* (Wigan, 1996)

Bateson, Walter, *The Way We Came: An Historical Retrospect of the Adventures of the Pioneers of the Amalgamated Society of Dyers* (Bradford, 1928)

Berger, Peter L., and Luckman, Thomas, *The Social Construction of Reality* (New York, 1966)

Bolton, Charles, *Salford Diocese and its Catholic Past* ([Salford?], 1950)

Briggs, Asa, *Victorian Cities* (London, 1968)

Busteed, M. A., '"The Most Horrible Spot"? The Legend of Manchester's "Little Ireland"', *Irish Studies Review*, no. 13 (winter 1995–96), pp. 12–20

—— and Hodgson, R. I., 'Irish Migration and Settlement in Early Nineteenth-Century Manchester, with Special Reference to the Angel Meadow District in 1851', *Irish Geography*, xxvii, no.1 (1994), pp. 1–13

——, —— and Kennedy, T. F., 'The Myth and Reality of Irish Migrants in Mid-Nineteenth-Century Manchester' in Patrick O'Sullivan (ed.), *The Irish World Wide: History, Heritage, Identity*, ii: *The Irish in the New Communities* (London & Leicester, 1992)

Davies, Andrew, and Fielding, Steven (eds), *Workers' Worlds: Cultures and Communities in Manchester and Salford, 1880–1939* (Manchester, 1992)

Dunleavy, J., 'The Irish Dimension of the British Labour Movement, 1886–1929', *North West Labour History*, no. 15 (1990–91), pp. 59–66

Dyer, Calico Printer, Bleacher, Finisher, and Textile Review, 1, no. 1 (1881)

Fielding, Steve, 'Irish Politics in Manchester, 1890–1914', *International Review of Social History*, xxxiii (1988), pp. 261–84

—— *Class and Ethnicity: Irish Catholics in England, 1880–1939* (Buckingham, 1993)

Fitzgerald, Mary Elizabeth, 'Catholic Elementary Schools in the Manchester Area during the Nineteenth Century' (M.Ed. thesis, University of Manchester, 1975)

Fitzpatrick, David, *Oceans of Consolation: Personal Accounts of Irish Migration to Australia* (Cork, 1995)

Hall, A. J., *Textile Bleaching, Dyeing, Printing and Finishing Machinery* (London, 1926)

Harris, Ruth-Ann, *The Nearest Place That Wasn't Ireland: Early Nineteenth-Century Irish Labor Migration* (Ames, Iowa, 1994)

Heimann, Mary, *Catholic Devotion in Victorian England* (Oxford, 1995)

Herbert, Michael, 'The Irish in Manchester', 1989 (typescript in Manchester Central Library)

Johnson, Paul, *Saving and Spending: The Working-Class Economy in Britain, 1870–1939* (Oxford, 1985)

Kay, Thomas Henry, 'The City I Knew', *Salford Local History Society Newsletter* (Feb. 1977)

Kidd, Alan, *Manchester* (Keele, 1996)

Lane, Peter, *The Catenian Association, 1908–1983: A Microcosm of the Development of the Catholic Middle Class* (London, 1892)

Lannon, David, 'Bishop Turner and Educational Provision within the Salford Diocesan Area, 1840–1870' (M.Phil. thesis, University of Hull, 1994)

Lowe, W. J., *The Irish in Mid-Victorian Lancashire: The Shaping of a Working-Class Community* (New York, 1989)

—— 'The Lancashire Irish and the Catholic Church, 1846–71', *Irish Historical Studies*, xx, no. 78 (Sept. 1976), pp. 129–55

McCaffrey, Lawrence J., *The Irish Diaspora in America* (Washington, DC, 1984)

Makepeace, Christopher, *Manchester As It Was*, iii: *Social and Industrial Life* (Hendon Hill, Lancashire, 1974)

'Memoir of Brother Ignatius of the Xaverian Institute', *The Harvest: An Organ of Catholic Works*, x, no. 118 (July 1897), pp. 148–50

Neil, Frank, 'Irish–English Conflict in the North-West of England: Economics, Racism, Anti-Catholicism, or Simple Xenophobia?', *North West Labour History*, no. 16 (1991–92), pp. 14–25

O'Toole, P. L., *History of the Clan O'Toole* (Dublin, 1890)

Roberts, Robert, *The Classic Slum: Salford Life in the First Quarter of the Century* (London, 1973)

Swift, Roger, and Gilley, Sheridan (eds), *The Irish in the Victorian City* (London, 1985)

Index